The Kid from Cuba:

Zoilo Versalles

OTHER DOUBLEDAY SIGNAL BOOKS

BONNIE
PONY OF THE SIOUX
THE JUNGLE SECRET
NORTH POLE:
  The Story of Robert Peary
BASEBALL BONUS KID
CAROL HEISS: *Olympic Queen*
GREEN LIGHT FOR SANDY
SEA TREASURE
THE BLOOD RED BELT
KENDALL OF THE COAST GUARD
RODEO ROUNDUP
NANCY KIMBALL, NURSE'S AIDE
FOOTBALL FURY
CIVIL WAR SAILOR
DINNY AND DREAMDUST
AUSTIN OF THE AIR FORCE
THE LONG REACH
FOOTLIGHTS FOR JEAN
BASEBALL SPARK PLUG
RUNAWAY TEEN
LIGHTNING ON ICE
HOT ROD THUNDER
JUDY NORTH, DRUM MAJORETTE
DIRT TRACK DANGER
ADVENTURE IN ALASKA
CLIMB TO THE TOP
FISHING FLEET BOY
JACK WADE, FIGHTER FOR
  LIBERTY
THE MYSTERY OF HIDDEN
  HARBOR
SCANLON OF THE SUB SERVICE
A SUMMER TO REMEMBER
NAT DUNLAP, JUNIOR "MEDIC"

BLAST-OFF!
  A Teen Rocket Adventure
TWO GIRLS IN NEW YORK
THE MYSTERY OF THE FLOODED
  MINE
CATHY AND LISETTE
EVANS OF THE ARMY
HIGH SCHOOL DROP OUT
DOUBLE TROUBLE
PRO FOOTBALL ROOKIE
THE MYSTERY OF BLUE STAR
  LODGE
ADVENTURE IN DEEPMORE CAVE
FAST BALL PITCHER
HI PACKETT: *Jumping Center*
NURSE IN TRAINING
SHY GIRL:
  The Story of Eleanor Roosevelt
SKI PATROL
BIG BAND
GINNY HARRIS ON STAGE
GRACIE
THREE CHEERS FOR POLLY
SECOND YEAR NURSE
FEAR RIDES HIGH
THE MYSTERY OF THE INSIDE
  ROOM
ARTHUR ASHE: *Tennis Champion*
MYSTERY OF THE THIRD-HAND
  SHOP
GOING, GOING, GONE
ROAR OF ENGINES
GANG GIRL
TV DANCER

The Kid from Cuba: Zoilo Versalles

BY JAMES TERZIAN

Doubleday & Company, Inc.
Garden City, New York

Contents

chapter		page
1	"A Very Small Cat"	9
2	The Try Outs	19
3	Major League Scout	32
4	Life in the Minors	43
5	Marriage, the Major Leagues, and Minnesota	53
6	"The Lonesome Latin"	69
7	Seasons in the Sun	81
8	Two Kids from Cuba	92
9	The Three-hundred Dollar Shower	101
10	Winning the Pennant	113
11	The Most Valuable Player	130

The Kid from Cuba:

Zoilo Versalles

CHAPTER 1

"A Very Small Cat"

Zoilo Versalles was born to baseball and poverty. The place of his birth was a one room hut in Marianao, a very poor section of Havana, Cuba. It had a straw roof, four small windows, and a bare clay floor.

On the day he was born, December 18, 1940, women of the neighborhood came to help, while the father, also called Zoilo, sat outside with his friends. As he waited, he argued about *beisbol*—baseball—the Cuban national game.

Other neighbors brought in gifts for the mother and child, ribbons and buttons and dolls they had made themselves. They were simple presents, for the people of Marianao had no money to buy gifts. They had little enough for food. Zoilo, senior, had not worked all month. But tomorrow, perhaps, his luck would change. There might be a ditch to dig or a field to clear—anything to bring in a little money.

An old woman finally walked out of the hut, her face all smiles. "A fine boy, *señor!* But he is so small—hardly bigger than the hand of a man. He will need much rice and beans to make him grow!"

Mr. Versalles sighed and dusted off his patched trousers. "One more mouth to feed," he thought. There never seemed to be enough food in the house. Or enough room. There was already another child, Lazaro, born three years before. And now this new baby. Still, the father smiled happily as he looked down at his wife, Amparo, and his new son. If there was a job anywhere within twenty miles, he would find it.

The Versalles family—the two little boys and their parents—all lived together in that small hut. They slept and ate there, and cooked their meals over a little stove under a window in one corner.

If the Versalles house was cramped, however, there was no lack of room in the dusty streets and alleys of Marianao, where Zoilo grew up, the smallest, skinniest kid in the neighborhood. Dark eyed, dark skinned, and barefoot, he tagged along behind Lazaro, a darting shadow to his older brother. Lazaro called him *"hermanito"* —little brother—and taught him the games of the street. He protected him from the older boys, too, and shared pieces of sugar cane with him.

On Zoilo's sixth birthday, an uncle gave him a small rubber ball. At the sight of the gift, the boy's big eyes grew even bigger. He held on to that ball as if it were something alive. And in his hands it *did* come to life. From then on, neighbors to the left and right of the Versalles hut heard the constant *dub-a-dub-dub* of the rubber ball, bouncing against a wall. If this annoyed some of the women, it only amused the men.

"Hey, Versalles," someone called out to Zoilo's father, "you got yourself a big league player in that boy, for sure. Look at him go after that ball. Like a cat after a mouse!"

"A very small cat," another added. "A big league mouse would eat him up!"

Little Zoilo heard the gentle laughter. It was not meant to be unkind, but he thought they were making fun of him. His small, pinched face grew hot with anger. He would show them some day!

It was just after his sixth birthday that Zoilo started going to the local public school in Marianao. However, the boy had little interest in words and numbers. He was far more anxious to get out and play with his rubber ball. And he was hungry—always hungry!

One day, when he was seven years old and in the second grade, Zoilo decided that being hungry was bad enough, but to have to sit through school, too, was more than he could stand. That day he had gone home for lunch with his brother Lazaro only to find that there was nothing to eat in the house.

"When your father comes home tonight, he will bring a chicken," Mrs. Versalles told them. Zoilo could see that it pained her to have nothing to feed them.

"He was called in for a day's work in the lumber yard." She continued, trying to cheer them up, "Now, wash your faces and go back to school, and I will make you a feast for dinner. I promise!"

Lazaro tightened his belt. He was used to that empty feeling in his stomach. "C'mon, Zoilo," he said, as he took his younger brother by the hand. "At least we have a good appetite for tonight, yes?"

Zoilo's face plainly showed his disappointment. He couldn't possibly sit still in class, with that gnawing pain tugging inside him. Half way to school he suddenly dropped his brother's hand. "I know where the lumber yard is, Lazaro. I am going to meet Papa to make sure nothing happens to that chicken!"

Zoilo ran off before Lazaro could stop him. No more of that school for him, Zoilo told himself, as he ran barefoot through the streets toward the lumber yard. "I will never go back." It seemed to Zoilo that the hunger was at its worst when he was there.

And just as he had decided, he never went back. "I do not feel well," he said the next day, when his mother tried to talk him into going. Another time he complained to her that he had no shoes, although few boys in the school did. And still another time, he refused to go because his trousers were ripped. What ever the reason, no one at home or in Marianao really seemed to care whether he attended classes or not. The poor in those days had much more to worry about than a formal education for their children.

Some days Zoilo went with his father in search of work. Some days he stayed at home to help his mother cook and clean. And some days, when no one was looking, he climbed over the wall of the big baseball stadium in Havana to see the game. He didn't mind going hungry then. In fact, he hardly ever thought about it when he was watching big league baseball

The boy's favorite team was the *Armendares* of the Cuban National League. When they lost, he went home in tears. When they won, his bare feet never even felt the dust of the streets.

But most of the time, young Zoilo could be found in an alley, playing with his rubber ball. *Dub-a-dub-dub!* He would scoop up the bouncing ball and throw it back at the wall, just as he had seen the big league players at the stadium do. And since baseball was his pride and passion, Zoilo taught himself to read, as he grew older, by slowly sounding out the names of teams and their players. His reader was the sports pages of the local paper. His arithmetic lessons were the won and lost records and batting averages.

When it was too hot—there are no winters in Cuba,

just one long season of sun—he sat in the shade and copied box scores. In this way he also taught himself to write. One day, he wet the stub of a pencil on his tongue and slowly wrote his own name at the top of the line-up.

"Zoilo Versalles," he wrote, "short stop." Then he put down the names of the other members of the *Armendares* nine.

By the time Zoilo had reached the age of twelve, he was fast enough for sand lot baseball, although he was still small. He played on local pick-up teams—there were no "little leagues" in his childhood. He borrowed a glove from an opposing player when ever the teams changed sides. His favorite position was short stop. His favorite player was Willie Miranda, a great star in the Cuban National League, and later a short stop with the New York Yankees and Baltimore Orioles. Miranda was a fine fielder but a weak hitter. The words "good field, no hit" might have been written just for him.

Zoilo patterned himself after his hero. Could Willie "go into the hole"—the deep area between the short stop's right and third base—and come up with a ground ball? Sure—so Zoilo went "into the hole." Could Willie dash in, scoop up a slow roller, and nail the runner at first? You bet he could—so Zoilo dashed in. Or he scampered to his left as Willie did, or ran out to the outfield for short pop flies, or covered second base on a steal.

At first his moves were awkward. But with Lazaro batting out grounders at him hour after hour, Zoilo soon learned to cover the left side of the infield like a blanket.

By the time he was fourteen, he had all the natural equipment for a short stop—a fine pair of hands, a good arm, keen eyes, and speed to burn. The only thing he lacked was a glove of his own. But gloves cost money, far more money than Zoilo's family could afford.

It was about this time that Lazaro paid his younger brother the supreme compliment. "Zoilo, you look like Willie Miranda. You field like him and you run like him. But," he added, "you had better learn to hit a lot better than Willie if you want to move up as a ball player. A skinny kid like you has to make up in brains what he doesn't have in power. Let's see you snap your wrists when you swing a bat. Like this!"

Lazaro whipped the bat around, much as a man playing golf does when he drives off a tee. The older brother was not nearly as good a player as Zoilo, but he was a keen student of the game. He taught his younger brother all that he had learned.

Zoilo swung again and again until Lazaro was satisfied. That snap of the wrists at the last second, timed perfectly to meet the ball, added great power to the boy's smooth, natural swing. The bat the brothers used was chipped, the baseball taped and out of shape, and the gloves—when they could borrow them—were strips of leather.

One day, when they came home after practice, they found their father talking to a tall, powerful-looking stranger. Both men were drinking *café negro*, the strong, black Cuban coffee. Mr. Versalles put down his cup. "My sons," he announced, "we have an honored guest."

They peered at the stranger. There was something familiar about that face—

"Boys, meet Carlos Paula."

Zoilo froze in his tracks. Carlos Paula, the baseball player! *That's* where he had seen that face—in the newspapers! Paula played the outfield for the Washington Senators and was also a big favorite in Cuban baseball. But what was he doing here, in Zoilo's own house?

"We knew each other as boys in Marianao," Mr. Versalles explained, "before Carlos became famous." He turned to his guest. "People around here say that we have a couple of future major league players right here in the family." He waved proudly toward his two sons.

Lazaro stepped back. "Not me. *Him!*" He pushed his younger brother forward. "Zoilo's the real ball player. I'm only the coach." Zoilo remained silent, his eyes big with wonder. "Well, say something, little brother. Short stops are supposed to talk it up!"

"Short stop, eh?" Carlos boomed. He had a voice to

go along with his powerful body. "That's a good position to choose. Not much chance of getting a sore arm, the way pitchers do." He held out his hand to the boys.

Zoilo could hardly believe it. A major league player was talking to *him*, shaking *his* hand! But the next moment he cried out in pain. "A bruise," he said. "My hands, they are sore from baseball."

"We played today without gloves," Lazaro explained. "Nobody showed up, so Zoilo fielded with his bare hands. Did pretty good, too."

Carlos Paula turned up the boy's palms. They were red and sore. "It is foolish to risk broken fingers, especially for someone who wants to be a big league short stop. How old are you, Zoilo?"

"Fourteen . . . going on fifteen!"

Just then Mrs. Versalles called them to dinner. But for the first time in his life, Zoilo paid no attention to food. He was thinking about something more important. He was thinking about baseball.

Next morning, Carlos Paula paid another visit to the Versalles family, this time to thank them for their kindness. Before leaving, he handed Zoilo a bundle wrapped in brown paper. "For you," he said, smiling. "No more sore hands, eh?"

The boy murmured his thanks shyly, almost afraid to guess what the package contained. It felt like—it looked like— He ripped it open with trembling fingers. It was! A real, full-size baseball glove!

"My old mitt," Carlos Paula explained. "Maybe you will have use for it, eh? And something else—" He held out a pair of spiked shoes. "I need a new pair, anyway. And for you, Lazaro, a couple of bats and a baseball, so you and your brother can practice better, yes? So now, *adios*, everybody. And good luck!"

Zoilo stared at his treasures. The mitt was worn, but soft and comfortable. It had been well broken in. The shoes were also used, and a couple of sizes too large. But never mind, they had real spikes on them!

Zoilo slipped the glove on his left hand, then made a quick stab, as if at a ground ball. Nothing would ever get past him again. And those spikes—why, he could run like the wind in them!

Lazaro was beaming. With these major league bats and the baseball, he and his brother would be the talk of the neighborhood.

When Zoilo went to sleep that night, a pair of newly polished baseball shoes rested at the foot of his bed. The glove, rubbed to a shine and smelling of oil, was tucked under his pillow.

CHAPTER 2

The Try Outs

From that day on, Zoilo always had his glove and spikes close by. They were his most precious possessions.

One afternoon his older brother stuck a copy of *El Diario*, a popular Havana newspaper, under his nose. "Try outs," Zoilo read. "The *Fortunas*, of the Havana Amateur League, will hold open try outs at City Park—on Saturday, April 15, 1955. All boys fourteen years or older—"

Zoilo counted on his fingers. "April 15, that's tomorrow! And I was fourteen last December. Lazaro, what are we waiting for?"

"You said it yourself—tomorrow! Take it easy until then."

Zoilo just couldn't. All night long he tossed and turned, woke up, polished his shoes, rubbed more oil into the glove, then fell back into a light sleep. The *Fortunas* were one of the best amateur teams in Havana! Did he stand a chance?

Next morning, with his glove and spikes under his arm, he and Lazaro set off for City Park, some ten miles from home. The bus from Marianao went directly there, but the boys could not afford the fare. "Besides," Zoilo thought, "the walk will strengthen my leg muscles."

Tired and hot, they arrived at the park. Hundreds of boys were swarming around the field. An important-looking man was telling them where to go. "Outfielders over there! Pitchers and catchers here! Infielders on the other side!"

"That's us," Lazaro said. "Get your spikes on, Zoilo."

The younger Versalles was already stuffing rags into the toes of his baseball shoes, so they would be snug on his small feet. With a final tug at the laces, he jumped up and ran toward a large group gathered around a heavy man wearing a baseball cap.

"That's Señor Rivera, the manager," Lazaro whispered. "You are in luck, little brother. He is going to look you over himself."

Señor Rivera waved a bat. "Fielding try outs first," he yelled. "All candidates for infield positions line up here. You," he turned to Lazaro, who, at seventeen, was among the tallest and biggest of the boys. "What's your position?"

"Oh, I am not trying out, señor. It is my brother. He plays short stop. And very good, too!"

The manager looked at Zoilo, who just came up to Lazaro's shoulder. "That runt? Why, he's not big enough to carry a glove. All right, the rest of you, let's go!"

A crowd of boys rushed out to the infield. When Zoilo finally made his way to the short stop post, he found himself at the end of a long line. "Get lost, kid!" one of the older boys said, elbowing him out of the way. "They are handing out lollipops over at the other end."

Zoilo's lips trembled. "I'm not a kid! I was fourteen last—"

Lazaro put a hand on his shoulder. "Take it easy, little brother. Save it for the ball game."

But Zoilo *was* small for his age, hardly five feet tall, and only a hundred pounds soaking wet. He could be passed over easily.

By this time, the first boy in line had stepped up to his position. *Señor* Rivera rapped a grounder at him. The boy ran to his left, scooped up the ball, and threw sharply to the first baseman. Zoilo followed every move closely. Could he do as well?

He noticed that the grounders were being hit harder and harder. The manager was an expert batter. He sent the fielder first to one side, then to the other, making each shot more difficult to handle. Some boys were called in after their try out, and their names were taken down by an assistant. "The lucky ones," Zoilo thought. The others were waved off.

Zoilo danced around at the end of the line, waiting impatiently for his chance.

The line grew smaller. Finally, he was the only one left.

"Okay!" the manager called out. "Now get over here and line up for batting try outs."

"But, *señor*—!" Zoilo ran in, tears in his eyes. "I have not had my chance!"

"You still here?" the manager said to Zoilo, then turned to Lazaro. "Why don't you tell that kid brother of yours to come back when he grows up?"

"Why don't you give him a chance?"

Rivera bit down hard on the stub of his cigar. "All right! I will give him a chance. Then we can get on with the batting try outs!"

He waved Zoilo back to his position, gripped the bat tightly and tossed the ball up in the air. *Bung!* A grass-cutting shot out to Zoilo's far right. Lazaro groaned. Not even Willie Miranda could have fielded that—!

But Zoilo had seen the anger in Rivera's eyes. He guessed the manager would try to make him look bad. So he was on his toes and flying as soon as the ball left the bat. With a desperate move, he stretched his gloved hand across his body, snagged the grounder, straightened up, and threw a straight peg to first.

"Lucky!" Rivera growled. "Let's see you get this one!"

Again the sharp crack of the bat. This time the ball

skipped toward second base. It would have bounced over the bag and into the outfield, except that Zoilo had figured the direction of the grounder. Scooping it up, he pegged it to first again, then trotted back to his position, trying not to look too pleased with himself.

The manager spat out his cigar. He took a deep breath, tossed the ball in the air, and swung hard. A bullet! The ball took a sharp bounce toward Zoilo, the hardest kind of shot for a short stop to handle. It was one that would get by any but the best of ball players.

"Charge it!" Lazaro yelled as the ball bounced.

Zoilo charged. He picked it up on the short hop. The force of it almost knocked him off his feet. Still, he recovered quickly, dug the ball out of his glove, and made the throw to first base.

Señor Rivera's mouth dropped open in surprise, then curved into a broad smile. He knew class when he saw it. "Okay, kid, you win." He tapped a slow roller that went past the pitcher's mound. Zoilo ran in, picked it up with his bare hand and whipped it over to the first baseman—all in one motion.

"Just like Willie Miranda," the manager's assistant called out.

After a few more grounders, all of which Zoilo fielded without error, the manager turned to Lazaro. "What did you say your brother's name was?"

"It is Zoilo. Zoilo Versalles."

23

"Write that down," the manager said to his assistant. Then he lit a fresh cigar. "Can he swing a bat as well as he can field?"

When batting try outs began, Zoilo was first in the box. "Bear down," he heard the manager call out to the mound.

Zoilo watched the pitcher wind up, and dug his spikes into the ground. He was still flushed with the good impression he had made in the field.

"Look out, Zoilo!"

Lazaro's cry and the pitch reached almost at the same time. Down he went as the ball flew past his head. They were pitching him tight, trying to scare him off the plate!

Zoilo picked himself up, brushed the dirt off his pants, and glared at the pitcher. The pitcher glared back. This time he threw a curve that cut the heart of the plate. It never passed it. Zoilo stepped in, snapped his wrists at the last possible moment, and felt the fat part of the bat meet the ball. *Smack!* Now it was the pitcher who hit the dirt as the ball shot past *his* head.

Zoilo tried to hold back a smile. Deck him, would he?

The pitcher, now showing a healthy respect for the young batter, pitched to the corners. But Zoilo had his number. He pulled inside pitches to left, poked outside pitches to right, and sent line drives whistling to center

24

on balls that split the plate. His hits were clean line drives. Lazaro had taught him well.

When the batting try outs were over, *Señor* Rivera called the Versalles brothers aside. "You are all right, kid," he said to Zoilo, "though where you get all that power from, in that skinny little body, I will never know. How would you like to play for the *Fortunas?*"

Zoilo almost fainted.

"You won't be a regular yet. You will do a lot of sitting on the bench for a while. Watch the older players and practice with them. And maybe put on some weight, eh? Report here next Saturday at nine and we will fit you for a uniform. You," he turned to Lazaro, "make sure he shows up."

"If I have to carry him all the way from Marianao on my back."

"No need for that. What's the matter with the bus?"

There was an embarrassed silence. "Oh, no, *señor.* We walk, like we did this morning," Zoilo said.

Rivera was stunned. "You *walked*—ten miles? All the way?"

"We do not have bus fare," Lazaro said, "but we come back next Saturday, for sure."

"Wait a minute." The manager dug into his pocket as he spoke. "I want my players fresh for practice, not worn out." He put several coins into Zoilo's hand. "Next time take the bus."

Zoilo stared down at the money. Two *pesetas*—about forty cents! He had never had so much money before. He grinned at his older brother. He hadn't yet played his first game of organized baseball and already it was beginning to pay.

The following Saturday, as promised, Zoilo was fitted for a uniform, the smallest there was. At that, it hung loosely from his slight frame. His thin little body simply could not fill it, no matter how much he puffed out his chest.

After infield drills, in which the newest member of the team took part, the manager called for a practice game. "You, Zoilo, start at short. And bat first."

The boy grabbed his mitt and raced over the infield grass. He rubbed a wet palm over the letters of the uniform. *His* uniform!

At bat he was almost as nervous as the opposing pitcher was wild. Zoilo took four balls without even lifting the bat off his shoulder, then trotted to first. Out of the corner of his eye, he saw the coach flash the signal for the hit and run.

Zoilo took off for second with the wind-up, his feet churning the base paths. He heard the sharp crack of the bat and saw the ball heading toward the hole between first and second. But the second baseman was also fast. Changing direction, he went to his left, and speared the grounder. Then he wheeled around for a force play on Zoilo, who was charging into second.

"Slide!" The coach yelled from the sidelines.

But Zoilo went into second standing up. He was an easy out.

Señor Rivera accepted the mistake calmly. "Maybe the boy does not know how to slide," he said to himself. There was much he would have to be taught.

"Why did you not slide into second, Zoilo?" he asked after the other team was retired. "Don't you know how?"

"*Si!* I slide good, *señor*. But not now. Not in my new uniform. I do not want to get it dirty."

The manager hid a smile. He, too, had once been a young ball player. He understood.

In the weeks and months that followed, Zoilo's uniform got plenty dirty—and even ripped. He got into the last few innings of games in which his club was either comfortably ahead or far behind. After each game, he took his uniform home and washed it himself.

One day, finding a small rip in his baseball shirt, he took it off the drying line and began to mend it. Suddenly his sewing was interrupted by a light laugh. Zoilo looked up to see Maria Josefa Fransillo, a girl who lived in the next block of huts. They had known each other since they were little children.

"And what are you laughing at?" he wanted to know.

Maria, two years younger than Zoilo, laughed again.

"You," she said. "You aren't very good with the needle and thread, that's for sure."

"I'm a ball player," he answered importantly. He held up his baseball shirt.

"I know," she answered. Her lovely face, the color of honey, was topped by a crown of jet black, braided hair. "I've seen you play."

He was immediately impressed. "You have?"

She nodded. "You play short stop much better than you sew. Here, let me do it for you." She took the needle and thread and began to mend the shirt, using quick, tiny stitches. After she finished, Maria bit off the thread and gave him back his shirt. "There!"

Zoilo thanked her. Girls, he knew, could cook and clean and sew, but here was one who could also talk baseball. And she had actually seen him play. A wild idea struck him. "Maria, would you—? Look, I got two tickets for the game next Sunday. Could you—" He stopped short, afraid she would turn him down.

"I would love to, Zoilo. But, first, I will have to ask my mother."

Next Sunday, while Zoilo rode the bench watching his team fall behind 10–3, Maria sat in the reserved section. From time to time, he stole a glance in her direction. She was sitting next to Lazaro, cheering for the *Fortunas*, in spite of the fact that they were losing.

At the top of the sixth inning, he heard his name

called out. "You, Versalles, go in at short!" It was *Señor* Rivera waving him off the bench.

Zoilo jumped up and dashed to his position. This was the earliest he had ever been put into a ball game. And with Maria watching—! A wave of laughter greeted his appearance on the field. Zoilo looked about. Had something gone wrong? Why was everyone laughing?

A glove—*his* glove—sailed off the bench. In his rush, he had taken the field without his mitt! What a way to break into the line-up! He pounded his glove, wondering how much Maria had seen.

The first batter in the top of the seventh hit a sharp grounder to short. Zoilo came in, fielded it easily, straightened up. But for one split second, took his eyes off first. He searched the stands for Maria, wondering if she had seen him field the ball. As a result, his throw was far over the first baseman's head, for a two-base error.

Zoilo bit his lip. He was playing like a kid! Showing off!

"Settle down!" the second baseman growled.

"Okay," he murmured. "We get the next one."

The "next one" was a hard shot, a line drive, almost directly over the pitcher's head. The runner on second took off for third, certain it would be a base hit. Zoilo also took off, gloved hand stretched forward.

With a ball player's sure feeling, he knew that he would never get to that line drive unless he threw himself at the ball. He did, leaving his feet. He felt the ball hit the pocket of his glove—one out! A moment later, he fell across second base for an eye-popping double play.

The stands cheered. Zoilo heard nothing but the pounding of his own heart. He got up and dusted off his uniform.

"That's the way!" The second baseman patted him on the rump with his glove. "Keep your eye on the ball."

Zoilo trotted back to his position. For the rest of the game he never once glanced over to where Maria was sitting, not even when the team changed sides. "The name of the game," he said to himself, "is baseball!"

Maria Josefa Fransillo never missed another game in which Zoilo Versalles played for the *Fortunas*. All that year and the next, while Zoilo worked his way up from the bench to become the team's regular short stop, she watched him play. She and Lazaro—and often Zoilo's parents and *her* own mother and father—traveled to the ball park to cheer for the little short stop from Marianao.

Zoilo, as a matter of fact, wasn't so little any more. He had, finally, begun to grow. He was five feet, five inches tall by his sixteenth birthday, and he added two more inches the following year. By his seventeenth birthday he had almost reached his full height of five feet, ten inches. But he was still very thin. He weighed no more than 120 pounds.

What he lacked in weight, he more than made up in speed and grace, however. He drew raves for his fielding where ever he played. "A fine glove man," local newspaper men wrote of him.

And when he whipped a thirty-one ounce bat around in his powerful hands, he sent the ball screaming to the outfield on a line. "A tough man to strike out," opposing pitchers agreed.

Zoilo was the talk of the Havana Amateur League in the winter of 1957. Batting well over .300 and fielding perfectly, he became the pride of Marianao.

His greatest fan was Maria. She and the handsome young short stop were now "going steady." It was common knowledge that some day the two young people would get married. But when that day would be depended on a man neither of them had ever seen.

His name was "Papa Joe" Cambria.

CHAPTER 3

Major League Scout

Joe Cambria was the baseball scout in Latin America for the Washington Senators. Called "Papa Joe" because of his pleasant smile and endless stock of wonderful baseball stories, Joe Cambria had helped many a scared young man to make the grade into organized baseball. He was especially successful after Branch Rickey broke the color line by bringing up Jackie Robinson to the Brooklyn Dodgers in 1947.

Some of the major league stars Joe Cambria discovered were Pedro Ramos, Camilo Pascual, Conrad Marrero, and Mike Fornieles, all pitchers, and outfielders Bobby Estalella and Carlos Paula. All of them played for Washington at one time or another.

No spot in Latin America was too far for Papa Joe to travel to, no team too small to scout. He knew that many a future star could be found in the sugar cane fields of Cuba and on the factory teams in Puerto Rico.

That's why he paid particular attention to a letter he received in the winter of 1957 from his old friend Pablo Rivera.

"I have a couple of prospects for you," the manager of the *Fortunas* wrote, "especially one seventeen-year-old named Versalles. Only thing is, he is so skinny, he can hide behind a bat. We play a double-header in Havana on the last Sunday of this month. Maybe you can take a look at him."

Cambria wrote back to say that he would try to take in at least one of the games, and somehow word of his visit got around. On the morning of the double-header, all of Marianao was buzzing with excitement.

"Did you hear? Papa Joe is coming to town!"

"To scout the *Fortunas!*"

"Somebody tell Zoilo!"

Nobody had to tell Zoilo. He and Lazaro had been talking about it all week. "If he signs me up," the young short stop said, putting on his uniform, "Maria and I can announce our engagement. And you and Papa can quit work—and we can all go live in America!"

"Take it easy, little brother," Lazaro laughed. "First you have to get the contract."

Zoilo grinned. His dark, handsome face, with its high cheekbones, strong straight nose, and flashing eyes fairly glowed with confidence. "Leave that to me, big brother! See you at the ball park. And when Cambria comes, give me a signal, okay?"

He ran for the bus, his glove and spikes tucked under his arm, his uniform freshly washed and proudly worn.

By game time, no one had yet seen the famous scout. "He will get here in time for the second game," Lazaro assured Zoilo. "I will let you know as soon as I spot him."

"Play ball!" the umpire yelled.

In that first game Zoilo played with an easy grace. He fairly sparkled in the field, making several marvelous stops and taking part in three double plays. At bat he was a terror, hitting a single, a double, a triple, and a home run in four times at bat. It was the finest day of his career, and the *Fortunas* whipped the opposition, 11–4.

"Better save something for the second game," Lazaro warned during the rest period.

"I'm just warming up. There's plenty more where that came from. I only wish—"

A buzz from the stands cut Zoilo short. He looked up just in time to see a well-dressed man make his way to a reserved seat in back of home plate. The man was far from young. His face was lined, his hair gray, and his shoulders slightly stooped, but he smiled broadly as he sat down. No doubt about it, this had to be Papa

Joe—anyone could tell from the fuss the crowd was making over him.

Manager Rivera confirmed it a moment later. "Give it all you have, Zoilo. I don't need to tell you who is in the stands today."

The short stop bounded out to his position. Here was his big chance, at last!

But suddenly he felt his knees buckle under him. His mouth went dry. His stomach turned upside down. The frightening thought that his every move would now be watched by a major league scout drained him of his confidence. Suppose something went wrong? Suppose he failed?

When the first batter came up, his mind was more on the visitor in the stands than on the game itself.

Crack! A hard shot came bounding toward him. Zoilo, still in a fog, moved toward the ball. He got a glove on it, but that was all. It rolled past him for an error.

A groan went up from the Marianao fans. Zoilo lowered his head and trotted back to his position. His ears were burning with shame. What a "bush" play—and right in front of Papa Joe!

The second batter poked a ground single to right, and Zoilo gave a sigh of relief that the ball hadn't come his way. Immediately he became angry with himself for thinking like that. Perhaps if the ball *had* been hit to him, he might have thrown the batter out.

The next batter bounced to the second baseman. With a man on first, Zoilo moved quickly toward the bag for what looked like an easy double play. The peg from his teammate was right on line. But the short stop was not. With his mind still on the error he had made earlier, he ran to the bag and passed it as he caught the ball. Momentarily, neither foot touched the base.

"Safe!" the umpire motioned.

To make matters worse, the runner slid into him, sending him to the ground. Usually, Zoilo would have taken the throw from the second baseman and touched the base for one out. Then he would have leaped high into the air to avoid the runner sliding in and flipped to first to complete the double play. Instead, he had been dumped on the seat of his pants, and both runners were safe. The official scorer called, "Error on Number 6," meaning the short stop.

Zoilo could have crawled into a hole, especially when the pitcher motioned for an infield conference. "Hey, Zoilo, are you all right?"

"Sure, sure, Miguel. I—I just wasn't thinking."

"Or thinking too much!" the pitcher growled. "Keep your mind on the field!"

Zoilo wasn't much better at bat. He walked, popped up, hit into a force play, and, in the last inning, took a called third strike with two runners in scoring position.

It was an altogether sorry performance by a player who was supposed to be showing himself off at his best.

As soon as he had made the last out, Zoilo hurried from the field, fighting back his tears. He had played the worst game of his life, and in front of Papa Joe Cambria! After a game like that, even Maria might turn him down!

Stumbling blindly toward the bus stop, he paid no attention to Lazaro, who was calling after him. Zoilo was in no mood to talk to anyone—not even Maria, who, he knew, would be waiting with Lazaro.

"Zoilo! Zoilo, over here!"

Zoilo kept going.

"Zoilo! Papa Joe wants to see you!"

That stopped him. All right, he would take his medicine. No excuses about being nervous or having butterflies in his stomach. He had just played a rotten game. Straightening his shoulders, he headed back to the bench, where Lazaro and Maria were waiting. Strangely enough, they were grinning broadly. Maria even planted a kiss on his dirty cheek. They were joined a moment later by Pablo Rivera, who almost swallowed his cigar in his excitement.

"He wants to see you, Zoilo! Papa Joe wants to come to your house and talk to your father!"

Zoilo's mouth dropped. "You are joking! After a game like that—"

"One of the best he's ever seen! That's what he said!"

"Now I know you are joking!" Zoilo was again close to tears. What a clumsy way to try and cheer him up. "Look, I played that second game as if I had lead in my pants and a hole in my head."

The manager and Lazaro looked at each other. Then they began to laugh. Even Maria joined in.

"What's so funny—?"

"You!" His brother could hardly contain himself. "Not the *second* game, Zoilo! The *first* game! Papa Joe saw the first game, from there." Lazaro pointed to a park building beyond left field. "Through field glasses. And he said—"

"He said," Rivera interrupted, "that in that first game you played the finest short stop he has ever seen in amateur ball. And he wants to sign you up. Tonight, if he can speak to your father."

The men sat quietly in a circle, Papa Joe, Mr. Versalles, and the two Versalles boys. Mrs. Versalles and Maria remained in the background serving *café negro*. Mr. Cambria was explaining the contract that he had spread out in front of Zoilo's father.

"Zoilo is not yet twenty-one, so you must sign for him, Mr. Versalles. That is, if you do not object."

"I am proud of my boy." The father beamed.

"He will make a fine short stop some day." The scout turned his eyes toward the young prospect. "Provided he keeps his mind on baseball. That's the way you get up to the major leagues, my boy. And that's the way you stay up there. Eat, sleep, and think baseball. Don't let anything interfere. Like this afternoon, in the second game. Oh, yes. You knew I was in the stands. And you were nervous, no?"

"Yes," Zoilo agreed, dropping his eyes.

"I knew you would be. That's why I scouted you in the first game, from a distance, through my field glasses. What I saw then was another Willie Miranda—only with power! But you still have much to learn, my boy.

"Maybe in five years, people will say Papa Joe has come up with another great short stop. *Maybe.* That's why I am recommending you for a try out with the Washington Senators next month in Florida. Now, Mr. Versalles, if you will sign here—"

Zoilo watched as his father signed on the dotted line. Next he put his own name down. He was glad now that he had taken the trouble to learn how to write.

With the signing out of the way, Mrs. Versalles served more coffee. "You will be given your airplane ticket to Orlando, and expense money for spring training," the scout went on. "You must bring your own glove and baseball shoes. The club supplies the rest, including return fare if you don't make the grade."

"Oh, but I will! I mean, I will try hard, *Señor* Cambria. No more stupid mistakes."

"I hope not. You've got everything it takes to make a great short stop. Eyes, arm, speed, and power. You are the best short stop prospect I have seen. But it will take time for you to develop into a major league player. Time, patience, and self-control." Mr. Cambria looked at his watch. "It is late, and I must be getting back to the hotel."

"And I must be getting home," Maria added. She stretched out an arm. "Zoilo?"

Hand in hand, the two young people went to the door. "They will get married some day, now that Zoilo has his contract," Zoilo heard his mother say to Joe Cambria.

Mr. Cambria got up to leave. "He is a fine boy, *Señora* Versalles, and a fine prospect. But he is not yet in command of himself."

"He will learn," Lazaro promised. "Zoilo is still a boy, just seventeen."

Three weeks later, in February of 1958, almost all of Marianao came out to the Havana air field to see their local hero off. Zoilo, dressed in his Sunday best, accepted flowers, presents, and good wishes. But underneath all the excitement, he felt a great sadness. For it was now time to say good-by, good-by to all his friends, good-by to his family, and, worst of all, good-by to Maria Josefa.

"I will miss you," he whispered, as she stood by his side.

"And I will miss you, Zoilo."

A loud speaker sounded: "Boarding for flight 722 to Orlando by way of Miami. Flight 722."

Zoilo turned to his mother. She was in tears. "Good-by, my son," she said. "Heaven keep you."

Zoilo looked down at his mother's tired face, her sad eyes. How hard she had worked for him. "I will send money home so that you will never again go hungry," he promised.

"Last call for flight 722," the loud speaker sounded again.

Zoilo picked up his bag, hugged his weeping mother, kissed Maria, shook hands with his father and Lazaro, and stepped out beyond the gate. He stopped as he put a foot on the steps that led to the inside of the plane. He had been so caught up in the excitement of the past few days that he hadn't even thought about the flight. It suddenly occurred to him that he had never been in the air before. Would he get sick, he wondered?

"Good-by, Zoilo! Good-by, my son!"

His mother's cry cut through the noise. He turned at the top of the steps, waved at her one last time, and stepped into the plane.

He was shown to his seat. As he leaned back, he could

hear his heart beating. To him it sounded even louder than the roar of the motors.

"Please fasten your seat belts."

Zoilo fumbled at the buckle. For one brief moment, he had the wild notion of dashing off the plane.

Then, *click!* The buckle snapped in place, and the ground began to roll under him. Zoilo gripped the arms of his seat. What was it Papa Joe Cambria had said? "—the best short stop prospect I have ever seen."

He hardly felt like that, not just then.

CHAPTER 4

Life in the Minors

It took less than two hours to fly from Havana to Orlando, Florida, by way of Miami. But to the seventeen-year-old Zoilo, it seemed like a journey into another world.

He had never before seen such a sight as the Senators' training camp. An enormous field, containing half a dozen baseball diamonds, stretched out before him. The grass was a bright green, the base paths smooth, the stands and surrounding buildings freshly painted.

After dinner Zoilo was assigned to a dormitory along with about thirty other rookies—new players. They all roomed together, country boys, big city hopefuls, college players—white, black, and brown. Because he spoke no English, Zoilo teamed up with Hilario Valdespino, another Cuban. Hilario—called "Sandy" for short—was a year older than Zoilo, and he knew some English. He had already played one year in the Senators' minor league farm system—the training ground for young professional ball players who lack experience.

Work outs began the next morning. As long as Zoilo was out on the diamond, as long as he was fielding and hitting and running the bases, he felt fine. But at night, after lights out, he began to think of home.

"It will be nice to go back next winter and tell the folks we played with major league ball players, *sí?*" Sandy Valdespino said to him from the next bed.

"*Sí,*" was all Zoilo could whisper.

He was issued his own uniform, a faded but clean outfit used by many rookies before him. How many had made the team, he wondered? And how many had failed?

He had little time to think during that first week. The coaches kept him on the run. There was much to do before the regulars arrived—physical examinations, baseball instruction, and drills.

"You will be given a complete try out," Washington manager Cookie Lavagetto told the rookies. "If you make the grade you will be assigned to a minor league team. If not—" He shrugged his shoulders. "So give it all you have."

Zoilo gave. He was the first on the field every morning, the last to leave in the afternoon. He hustled through every work out, whether it was exercise, fielding drills, or batting instruction. Although he didn't understand more than a couple of words of English, he could tell by the glances of the coaching staff that he was being closely watched.

Zoilo felt especially good prancing around short stop. He drew many admiring looks for his fielding. After the first couple of days, he lost much of his shy feeling, at least on the field. His glove did all the talking for him during practice games. Playing short stop, it was almost as if he hadn't left home at all.

One night after dinner, Zoilo and Sandy wandered into the dormitory recreation room, where a group of players had gathered around a TV set. They were watching *The Adventures of Zorro*, a popular program about a masked bandit of old Mexico, who was really a Robin Hood in disguise. Zoilo liked TV because it helped him learn English. He could already use such words as "money," "dinner," "mail," "laundry," and "how much?"

"Hey, here he comes now," one of the rookies said, as Zoilo sat down in front of the set. " 'Zorro' himself!"

Zoilo looked around, puzzled. Valdespino poked him in the ribs. "He means you," he said in Spanish. "They think your first name is Zorro, like that *hombre* on TV!"

The young short stop frowned. "No Zorro! *Zoy*-lo! *Zoy*-lo Ver-*sigh*-yes!" he insisted, pronouncing it slowly and correctly.

The other players smiled. "The way you play short

stop," one of them said, "you are a bandit, just like Zorro —stealing base hits from everybody."

"That's right," another agreed. "Call him Zoilo or Zorro, it makes no difference. That kid from Cuba is a real bandit with the glove."

The name stuck. Even though there were several other Cubans in camp, everyone knew who "the kid from Cuba" was—Zoilo Versalles, sometimes called Zorro.

The ranks of young hopefuls thinned out as the Washington regulars arrived for spring training. But the kid from Cuba stayed on, impressing everyone with his fielding and hitting. Although he and the other rookies drilled off by themselves, it was still a big thrill for Zoilo. He often stopped to stare at such big league players as Harmon Killebrew, Camilo Pascual, Chuck Stobbs, and Jim Lemon.

Zoilo wrote home every couple of days. His letters were full of news from training camp. He told of the players he met, the strange American food he ate— "there is so much of it, I have already gained three pounds"—and how much he missed everyone, especially Maria Josefa.

But his happiest letter came at the end of March, 1958. "I have made it!" he wrote. "*Señor* Lavagetto has assigned me to a team in some place called Elmira. I report next week. Meantime, tell Papa to be sure and sign my contract when it comes home." He signed the letter, then added a P.S. "My salary is not possible to believe. I will make 175 dollars a month—in American money!"

Zoilo's education began soon after he left the training camp.

Elmira was in the New York-Pennsylvania circuit. It was a Class D minor league, the lowest spot in professional baseball, except for the rookie winter circuits. The team was made up mostly of raw players like Zoilo, together with a few older men who were on their way out as active players. There were eighteen men on the team. They traveled from town to town in an old yellow bus that the team owners had picked up from the Elmira school system. In addition to the players, the club carried a manager, a coach, and a traveling secretary. These three individuals also served as bus driver, training coach, public relations man, pay master, short order cook, and equipment man, as the occasion demanded.

It was a big change from the organized ways of the training camp to the catch-as-catch-can struggle of minor league existence. Zoilo slept in third-rate hotels. He ate in cheap restaurants. He learned to fill up on pizza pie and milk. He pressed his own clothes.

His salary of 175 dollars a month, which had once seemed so magnificent, slipped away before his eyes. There were a number of expenses he hadn't counted on:

47

Federal and state income taxes, social security taxes, locker room fees, and other charges that cut deep into his salary. Also, as promised, he sent money home regularly. At the end of every pay period he had hardly enough left for a haircut, a movie, or a new glove and baseball spikes, which he had to pay for out of his own pocket.

The important thing to Zoilo, however, was that he was playing baseball. And playing it as though his very life depended on it!

The New York-Penn league started its season early in May. By the end of the month, the skinny kid from Cuba who roamed the infield for the Elmira club was the talk of the circuit.

"Versalles is batting over .300 and fielding well," scouts reported back to farm director Sherry Robertson. "However, he is something of a scatter-arm. Some of his throws sail so far over the first baseman's head, they wind up in the stands."

"Tell the manager to work on him," Robertson wrote back.

Zoilo warmed up with the weather. In June, after Elmira had played each of the other five clubs in the league, he had raised his batting mark to .340. "If he keeps this up," the team manager told his coach one night during a long bus ride to Erie, Pennsylvania, "the Senators will call him up by August 1."

Then one evening, just before going out to the ball park—most games were played at night—Zoilo got a cable from home. His mother was dead.

He couldn't believe it. Dead? He hadn't even known she was sick! A kind club secretary gave him a few days' leave to fly to Cuba for her funeral.

Zoilo came back to Elmira a quiet young man. He tried to play up to his old form, but he could not get his mind off his mother. "Perhaps," he said to himself, "if I had been home, she might still be alive now."

His batting average fell, his fielding suffered. "Look, kid," the manager finally said to him, "you got to snap out of it or the club will slip into the cellar and you with it. By the way, I fixed it with the boss so that your girl friend can call you from Havana tonight, collect!" Zoilo's spirits rose immediately. "After the game," the manager added.

That night the kid from Cuba sparkled. He rapped out two doubles and a single and scored three times to lead his team to a 9–4 victory over Hazelton. Then he hurried back to the hotel for Maria's call.

By mid-season Zoilo had gained back some of his form. The New York-Penn league played a short schedule of 128 games and the season was due to end just after Labor Day. After that, Zoilo knew, he would be on his way home. "Only eight more weeks to go!" he said to himself. He began to mark off the days on his calendar.

Then, in the final week of the campaign, Zoilo got a surprise. The Elmira papers carried the big local news: "Versalles Named Rookie of the Year! Kid from Cuba Honored by Sports Writers!"

In Washington, farm chief Robertson read the first year record of the seventeen-year-old short stop. Games played—124; times at bat—497; runs scored—71; hits—145; batting average—.292, fifth best in the league. His extra base hits included eighteen doubles, seven triples, and five home runs. He had also stolen nineteen bases.

"Versalles has everything to make him a big league player," the farm director wrote in his report—"speed, power, and fielding ability." Then he added: "Everything but age. He's still a kid."

Zoilo returned to Cuba a hero—in Marianao, at least. Although his mother's death still troubled him, he was delighted to see Maria again, and his brother and father. He brought back gifts for everyone, including several old baseball gloves for the young boys in the neighborhood.

Lazaro looked him over happily. "Little brother, you have put on weight. At least, I can now see your shadow. Yes, you have changed."

Cuba had also changed. Political pressure had forced Cuban leader Batista to resign on January 1, 1959. The following day, the man who helped put him out of office, a young revolutionary leader named Fidel Castro proclaimed a new president.

At first, there was general good feeling among Cubans about the change. But within months, it became obvious that Communist groups were in control of the new government.

"I don't like it," muttered Zoilo, as he prepared to leave for spring training in March. "Maria, let's get married now and leave for the United States together."

"I cannot," she protested. "I have not yet finished high school. Please let's wait until then."

Zoilo agreed. But once more his attention was divided between baseball and home.

The kid from Cuba was promoted to Class B ball that spring, and sent to Fox Cities, in Wisconsin. The Fox Cities team was in the "Three-Eye League," called that because in the old days teams in that league came from Indiana, Illinois, and Iowa.

Competition was greater in Class B ball. Players were older. Pitchers threw harder, runners ran faster, hitters hit farther. But Zoilo met every challenge head on. As the team's regular short stop, he batted a solid .278 for the season, including nineteen doubles, two triples, and nine home runs. And at the mid-season break, he was named the starting short stop in the Three-Eye League's All-Star game. Yet there was one thing wrong with

Zoilo's performance. He made thirty-four errors in the field that season, the most in the league.

"He has a fine arm," team coach Ellis Clary wrote to Washington, "but he guns the ball a mile over the first baseman's head. One thing I will say for Versalles, he has all the tools. But he has so many bad fielding habits that it is like teaching an alligator how to play the piano."

"In that case," Robertson wrote back, "let's call him up and work on him."

When Fox Cities finished its schedule on Labor Day, Zoilo was told that he was being assigned to Washington for the month of September. "The boss wants to take a close look at you, kid," Clary told him. By now, Zoilo could follow English pretty well without help. "You've got a month to show what you can do. Good luck!"

Zoilo received the news of his promotion with mixed feelings. He had counted on returning to Cuba as soon as possible. But here was his big opportunity—a chance to break into a big league line-up!

For a break like that, even going home could wait.

CHAPTER 5

Marriage, the Major Leagues, and Minnesota

Zoilo knew he was in the major leagues the minute he joined the Senators in Chicago for the opening of a four-game series against the White Sox. He checked in at a large hotel, ate in a first-class restaurant, and slept two in a room.

"You start at short tomorrow night," manager Cookie Lavagetto told Zoilo when he arrived. "Get a good night's sleep."

Zoilo tried, but without much success. He was nervous, worried about the impression he would make. All night long he roamed the short stop post in his imagination. And he saw himself in the batter's box, swinging at major league pitching for the first time in his life.

By game time that evening, however, the comfortable feel of bat, ball, and glove helped settle him down. As

53

he stood at attention for the "Star-Spangled Banner," he rolled his eyes slowly from side to side, gazing at the big banks of lights, the huge ball park, the large crowd, the press box, the four umpires, the stars in both dug outs, all big time. Now he was a part of it, if only for one brief month.

"We have a new face in the line-up tonight, folks," Halsey Hall, who did the radio broadcast for Washington, announced, "Zoilo Versalles, the kid from Cuba. Only eighteen, the Senators expect great things from him. And they will get them, too, if he plays anywhere near up to his minor league record."

Chicago that year was driving for the pennant. The Senators were in the cellar, going nowhere. They could afford to play a green hand at short, just to see what kind of material they had down on the farm.

In his very first time at bat, Zoilo batted in the number eight slot and singled sharply to left. Immediately he stole second. A big grin split his face as he dusted off his uniform. Playing in the big leagues didn't seem so tough, after all!

He learned quite the opposite as time went on. To his dismay, he saw that pitchers threw with far more control than in the minors, cutting corners with many kinds of curves. He was fooled more than once as the Senators dropped three out of four to the White Sox.

Then the team moved on to Detroit, with Zoilo just about holding his own at short.

Versalles had his best series in New York, playing against the New York Yankees. Twice he went deep into the hole to rob the great Mickey Mantle of what looked like sure base hits. Each time the Yankee star threw him a look of surprise as Zoilo gloved the ball and gunned it to first. "Where did *he* come from?" Mickey seemed to be saying.

His greatest thrill came in the get away game at Yankee Stadium, when he stepped into a Whitey Ford curve and sent it screaming on a line into the left field boxes. It was the first home run of his major league career. The Senators won that game, 4–2.

"I wish I could have had that ball back, Maria," he wrote home when the team returned to Washington. "I would have saved it for you."

The rookie got into twenty-nine games that September, but managed only nine hits in fifty-nine times at bat for a disappointing .153 batting average. It was good enough, however, for farm director Sherry Robertson. At the end of the season Zoilo was given a new contract with a raise in salary and the promise that he would be moved up to Charlotte, North Carolina, then in the Class A South Atlantic League.

Zoilo returned to Cuba in the fall of 1959 and found that the political picture had taken a turn for the worse.

The new Cuban president, in office only six months, had resigned in protest after charging that Communists had taken over the new government. Fidel Castro was calling the shots.

Zoilo was all for moving his family and Maria out of the country then and there. But his father refused. "What would I do in America? We know no one there. At least here I have a job." He had been working steadily in the lumber yard near Marianao. Lazaro had also found work, in a downtown department store. "Things will get better," Zoilo was told. "No need to run."

Maria Josefa was of the same opinion. "I have only a little more than a year of high school left. We will talk of the future after graduation, yes, Zoilo?"

He finally agreed and went about his business: playing baseball in Havana's winter league, where he became a great favorite. Then, early in 1960, he packed his grip once more for another round of spring training in Orlando, Florida.

In spite of being told that he would be Charlotte's regular short stop, Zoilo could not work up much enthusiasm for the job. His thoughts were of Marianao.

When a bad cold put him to bed for a couple of days, he seemed to lose all interest in baseball. "I am miserable," he wrote to Maria. "I lie in bed all day thinking of how nice it would be to be home again."

"Don't do anything foolish," Maria wrote back. But

56

Zoilo never got the letter. By the time it arrived at Orlando, he was on his way to Cuba. He had jumped camp, baseball's greatest sin!

Still, the Senators forgave him. Realizing that the rookie was lonesome for home, they cabled him return fare on condition that he bear down and pay close attention to baseball.

"You must do as they say, Zoilo," urged Papa Joe Cambria, who had been put on his trail. "They have invested a great deal in you. It is only fair to give them—and yourself—a chance to live up to their high hopes for you."

Maria was also firm. "No marriage, absolutely not, unless you go back," she insisted.

When he returned to Orlando, the rookie was immediately summoned to the office of Calvin Griffith, the tall, husky president of the ball club. "We believe in you, Zoilo. We believe you have a great talent and a fine future. You must believe it, too. Next time you have a problem, don't brood over it. Come talk it over with me. My office is always open to you. Will you remember that?"

Zoilo nodded. He was grateful for the owner's understanding. And grateful, too, that he hadn't been fined, the usual punishment for jumping camp. "I play, *Señor* Griffith. I do my best."

He was as good as his word. For the rest of the train-

57

ing season, Zoilo's fielding was great, his batting was good, and he was a terror on the base paths.

Playing Class A ball, he was the picture of grace, as he flashed across the diamond, robbing batters of base hits left and right. He soon got a reputation as the best glove man in the South Atlantic League. His throwing, however, continued to give him trouble, and he wound up the season with forty-two errors.

He also developed into a feared batter. Zoilo showed tremendous power at the plate, in spite of the fact that he weighed only 135 pounds. With fine muscles and a trim waist, he leaned into pitches with that smooth swing taught him years before by his brother.

In that summer of 1960, playing a full season, Versalles knocked out 154 hits in 139 games, for a tidy .278 batting average. He had hit thirty-three doubles, twelve triples, and eight home runs.

For his skill with glove and bat, he was named the league's All-Star short stop. It was getting to be a habit with him.

"This could be his year," farm director Robertson said. "Now, if we can only do something about that crazy arm of his!"

That was about the only bad thing coaches could say of the nineteen-year-old short stop's performance. For some strange reason, Zoilo got off a wild peg every once in a while.

"I don't know," he said one day after a work out. "Sometime the ball, she sails, zoom! Like she got a motor, huh?"

At the end of the season, Zoilo was called up once more by the parent club. But again major league pitching proved too much for the slight young man. He batted only .133 in fifteen games, getting just six hits in forty-six times at bat. But of the six safeties, two were doubles and two triples.

"He could be our next short stop," manager Cookie Lavagetto said at the close of the 1960 campaign.

The winter of 1960–61 was the winter of the big change for the Washington ball club, for Zoilo Versalles, and for Cuba.

The situation on the island had become more and more dangerous as Castro increased his hold on the nation. The bearded leader had seized all private industry and brought it under control of the central government, including millions of dollars in American business properties. Meanwhile, more and more people who did not agree with him were beginning to disappear.

In the face of all this, Zoilo Versalles and Maria Josefa Fransillo decided to get married. They were wed on February 2, 1961, just after his twentieth birthday and her eighteenth.

"Now we go to the United States together," he told

his pretty young wife. She agreed. "And we bring your family and mine with us, Maria, so you will not be alone in the new country."

But the Castro government had different ideas. All travel out of Cuba had been sharply reduced. It was all right for Zoilo to leave, since he already had a job in the United States, but his new wife could not. "It will take time to get her out," a Cuban official told him. "Have a good season, *Señor* Versalles." Whatever their political feelings, many Cubans still remained great baseball fans.

"I will join you as soon as I can get my travel papers," Maria promised at the air field. "Good-by, my husband. Take care of yourself."

Sadly and reluctantly, Zoilo climbed aboard the plane. How could he keep his mind on baseball with Maria so far off? He arrived in Orlando an unhappy young husband—without a wife.

The changing baseball scene kept him in line. Zoilo was given a contract for $7,000 a year, the lowest big league salary for rookies. It meant he would be eating and traveling first class, however, provided he also played that way. He made up his mind that he would, if only for his wife's sake.

Enormous changes were under way in the major leagues as well as in Cuba. Zoilo's old Washington club had now become the Minnesota Twins. Calvin Griffith had moved his team to Minneapolis-St. Paul, which meant that now Zoilo and his teammates would be playing out of the Twin Cities, instead of the nation's capital. The Senators, however, still remained in Washington. They were a new and different American League ball club.

The junior circuit had expanded to ten clubs in 1961 with the addition of the Twins in Minnesota and the Los Angeles Angels—later known as the California Angels. The National League was to follow suit the following year when the New York Mets and the Houston Colts—later called the Astros—were added to the senior circuit.

Zoilo worked hard that spring, encouraged by news that Maria was due to leave Cuba any day. As spring training drew to a close he had the short stop job pretty well sewed up. No other candidate could bat with his authority or cover as much ground. But once in a great while he still tossed the ball high over the first baseman's head.

"Watch every move he makes on the field," manager Lavagetto warned his coaches. "Let's see if we can find out why he throws that way every so often."

They watched like hawks, but they had no answer for it. Neither did Zoilo himself.

The Twins opened the 1961 season on April 11 against

the Yankees in New York. It was a raw and chilly day. But to sports editor Charles Johnson of the Minneapolis *Star and Tribune*, it was a day to remember. It was a day that "will live in the history of the American League as the start of major league baseball in . . . the Upper Midwest," as he wrote in his column that day.

And it was a day for rookie Zoilo Versalles to remember, too.

Leading off, he faced Whitey Ford. Ford was the pitcher Zoilo had hit his first home run off the year before. This time, however, Whitey had Zoilo's number, and Zoilo flied out to center as the Twins went down in order in the top of the first.

Taking the field, Zoilo felt a warm glow, in spite of the twenty-mile-an-hour wind blowing in across the field behind him. He had finally made it as the team's regular short stop. He picked up a practice ground ball and whipped it over to first base where another rookie, big Don Mincher, was holding down the bag. To his right, at third, was Harmon Killebrew, the feared "Killer" whose thirty-one home runs the year before placed him among the game's leading batters. Billy Gardner was stationed at second base. Pedro Ramos was on the mound, cool and full of confidence.

Zoilo wished he felt as calm. The truth was that his stomach was churning, his fingers tingling, his mouth dry in spite of a big wad of gum. He glanced over at the boxes behind the visitors' dug out where several of the Twins' wives were sitting. If only Maria Josefa were here!

Bobby Richardson stepped into the batter's box for the Yankees. After taking a called strike he hit a ground ball toward second. Zoilo rushed over, gloved the ball with one hand, and tossed out the runner. The peg was hard and true. His muscles loosened, his stomach stopped turning over. He had made his first play perfectly. The season was on!

The score was still o–o, as Zoilo came up for his second turn at bat in the top of the fourth. Whitey Ford blew on his fingers. The cold seemed to be bothering him. The first pitch was low and away. It might have been called a strike, except that Zoilo "rode with the pitch"—that is, he swung in the direction the ball was moving—and smashed it over the second baseman's head for a clean single.

"Hold her steady," first base coach George Strickland warned him. "Ford's got a sneaky move to first." Ford did, perhaps the best in the business. So Zoilo was surprised when Strickland flashed the steal sign on the very next pitch.

He dug his spikes into the base path the moment Whitey wheeled toward the plate. Second base, small and white against the brown infield dirt, seemed ninety miles away, instead of ninety feet. As he raced toward the bag, Zoilo saw Bobby Richardson brace for the throw. Zoilo slid in, hooking the bag with his left toe.

"Safe!" The umpire's palms swept downward.

Zoilo was delighted. He had stolen a base off Ford! Who would have thought it possible?

The flushed rookie glanced at the score board—one down. He studied the pitcher, while batter Lennie Green took a ball, then fouled off the next pitch. Ford, struggling against the cold, seemed to be thinking only of the batter. Sam Mele, the third base coach, was talking it up, but hadn't given any sign to steal yet.

Zoilo edged off the base. If Ford gave him the chance— He broke for third with the wind-up, getting a big jump on the ball. He was under third baseman Clete Boyer's glove well before the snap throw from catcher Elston Howard reached the bag.

"The kid from Cuba has done it again!" Mel Allen, who announced the Yankee games on TV, exclaimed in surprise. "Stolen another base off Ford! How about that?"

Zoilo's move paid off when Lennie Green sent a long fly to the outfield. The young short stop scored easily after the catch, giving the Twins their first run. He got another hit in the top half of the sixth, and Minnesota went on to humble the mighty Yankees 6–o, as Ramos pitched a neat six-hitter. The Twins, led by a rookie short stop and a smart veteran pitcher, had won the opening game of the 1961 season!

With the next game rained out, the team traveled to Baltimore, where the young short stop again raised eyebrows with his sharp play. Leading off at the top of the fourth, he sent a line drive to left center for a base hit. When the fielder was just a bit slow in picking up the ball, he turned on the speed and slid into second for a double. Zoilo scored moments later on an error by Oriole first baseman Jim Gentile.

In the seventh, with the score tied 2–2, Zoilo came to bat with a man on second, and singled in the go-ahead run. The Twins won 3–2, with the victory going to Camilo Pascual. As Minnesota sports writers gathered in the locker room after the game, a smiling Cookie Lavagetto pointed to the kid from Cuba.

"I found my short stop!" he proudly announced.

Zoilo made his manager look good as the Twins dumped the Orioles in a Sunday double-header, 10–5 and 6–4. The victory in the second game came on a two-run home run by Versalles in the top of the eleventh. The team followed with a 3–2 win over the Boston Red Sox in a series cut short by rain and cold. Then the Twins headed back home—in first place, with a record of five wins against a single loss.

Even more remarkable was Versalles' hitting record on the first road trip of the season. The kid from Cuba, who wore a Number 2 on the back of his uniform, had collected eleven base hits in his twenty-three at bats for an eye-popping .478 average.

Nevertheless, Zoilo was deeply troubled that spring, when a daring group of Cubans tried to overthrow the Castro government. He and other players from the Caribbean played that week with their attention divided between baseball and the military moves carried on in an area of southern Cuba known as the Bay of Pigs.

Though this took place far from Marianao, all of Cuba had been placed under alert by Castro. Zoilo immediately went to see Calvin Griffith. "I'm worried," he told him. "I have my father there, a brother, and my wife."

The club owner immediately called a meeting of all Cuban players. "I will do everything I can to find out about your relatives," he assured them. "So far, we have no word other than what you yourselves have heard over radio and TV."

The Bay of Pigs, as it turned out, was a sorry attempt to throw out Castro. Within a few days, the Cuban leader had brought the island completely under his control again.

"All is well with your families," Griffith was able to report to Zoilo and other Latin Americans on the team after forty-eight hours. "I've arranged with the Red Cross

66

for an open telephone line to Havana, so that you may talk with your relatives."

Zoilo spoke to his brother that night. Lazaro assured that things were calm in Marianao. "Keep your mind on baseball, little brother. We are all well."

Feeling much better, the rookie arrived with the rest of the team at the Twin Cities air field on April 20, 1961. There five thousand fans greeted them, even though it was the middle of the night. Zoilo blinked in surprise as perfect strangers singled him out, shook his hand, slapped him on the back.

"Boy, it was never like this in Washington," Harmon Killebrew grinned. "We are home, and I do mean home!"

The Twins stayed at the top of the league or close to it for the rest of the month. Then on April 30, in a home game against the Chicago White Sox, Zoilo went deep into the hole, reached for a batted ball, speared it in his glove—and failed to straighten up. The runner legged it out for a hit, while the short stop remained doubled over, a sharp pain spreading like fire at the base of his spine.

"Time!" third base coach Mele called out.

He was the first to reach the short stop. One look at the young man's face told the unhappy story—Zoilo Versalles had wrenched his back.

X rays showed nothing. "A severe muscle wrench," said

team physician Doctor William Proffitt. "You will have to take it easy for a week or so."

With Versalles out of the line-up, the Twins lost six out of their next seven games and just stayed above the .500 won and lost mark. The short stop returned to action on May 7, got two hits and stole two more bases. But the Twins lost 11–9 to the Red Sox, and fell five games off the pace.

"No pitching," manager Cookie Lavagetto growled. "We need tighter pitching to stay in competition." He glanced over the team's individual records. "Tighter pitching and a healthier Zoilo Versalles at short. As long as he stays in the line-up we have a chance."

Zoilo continued to play in spite of his aching back. He said nothing about it. He didn't want to be benched, not at the start of his first season as a regular. Besides, he didn't like being idle. When he wasn't in action he brooded constantly about home and about Maria. So pain or no pain, he decided to play.

CHAPTER 6

"The Lonesome Latin"

One of Zoilo's big problems at this time, although he didn't know it then, was his failure to eat properly. He missed his native dishes—rice and beans, chicken, and green bananas. The closest things he found to Cuban cooking were fried foods, so he ate those until his stomach protested.

One morning, toward the middle of May, he reported to Doctor Proffitt with severe stomach cramps. After a series of tests, the team physician spoke to club owner Griffith. "Something is definitely wrong with the boy."

"Sure it is not all in his mind?" Mr. Griffith knew something was bothering the young short stop. "I expect he's worried about his wife. Right now I'm doing everything I can to get her out of Cuba, but it isn't easy to deal with Castro's government, not after the Bay of Pigs."

"The kid worries all right," Doctor Proffitt agreed.

"But I think he's also sick. Let's keep a close watch on his diet, Cal."

Zoilo returned to the line-up after a couple of days on the bench. But he failed to spark the team. On May 26, the Twins played in Washington, D.C., their old home town. It was their first trip there since they left that city, and the team was greeted by a loud chorus of boos.

Versalles flushed. Why were they booing *him?* He was so upset that he made three errors, allowing two runs to cross the plate. It never occurred to him that the fans were angry at Cal Griffith and the Twins for having deserted them. Minnesota lost, 4–3, then went on to drop two more to the Senators, as Washington fans jeered in delight.

The reasons for the team's failure were not hard to pin point. Zoilo, at short stop, was ailing. Also, his mind was on every scrap of news that came out of Cuba. Others on the team were not playing well either. Rookie Don Mincher was having trouble at first and scarcely hitting his weight, while Billy Gardner had definitely slowed at second. With the infield full of holes, the pitching fell apart. The Twins lost six games in a row.

Trade talk filled the air. On June 1, reserve infielder Billy Consolo was traded to Boston for Billy Martin, the second baseman who had once played so well for the New York Yankees. The trade settled Zoilo down, and the young short stop's game improved greatly with Martin as his partner.

"He's a terror at short," Martin told manager Lavagetto. "That kid can do so many things so well—if only he would keep his mind on the game!"

Several days later, infielder Bernie Allen joined the team, just after his graduation from Purdue University. A star in sports at college, he came highly praised as an infielder. Julio Becquer, a Cuban first baseman, was also added to the Twins line-up.

Nothing helped. The Twins lost their ninth straight game on June 4. It was their twelfth out of the last thirteen. Three days later, after a 5–1 loss to the Yankees, they dropped into the cellar.

Cal Griffith called Cookie Lavagetto home for talks. Sam Mele, who coached third base for the Twins, took over the reins in Cookie's absence. Griffith told the press that it would only be for a short time.

News men, however, had their own ideas. "The club," one sports writer remarked, "is snake-bitten. The Twins are falling apart."

The word that the press had been expecting came on June 23—Sam Mele had been named manager of the Twins in place of Cookie Lavagetto.

Sam—his full name was Sabbath Anthony Mele—was a former major league outfielder, whose sad face and graying hair made him look older than his thirty-eight years. A quiet, pleasant man, he was, as Tom Briere of the Minneapolis *Tribune* put it, "well liked by the players."

He was respected by them as well. "Everybody is going to work every minute of every game," Sam told the team before game time on June 23. "We may not be the best club in the league, but, by golly, we are going to work harder than the rest!"

Zoilo took the words to heart. Playing in Yankee Stadium that night, he got two hits and brought the fans to their feet with an exciting bit of base running. After singling in the fifth, he took off for second on a hit and run play. Batter Bill Tuttle grounded to third, but Zoilo had such a jump on the ball that Yankee third baseman Boyer had no chance for the double play. Instead, he threw to first to get Tuttle. Meantime, Zoilo, running all the way, rounded second, and kept going. He stole third under the surprised noses of the Yankee infield. He later scored, as the Twins went on to shut out the Yankees, 4–0. It was their first win over New York since opening day.

"That's the way to move," Mele told Zoilo after the ball game. "Keep it up."

Zoilo had good reason for feeling peppy, especially when Calvin Griffith told him a few days later that Maria had just been given permission to leave Cuba. All

[1] Zoilo Versalles: The "Kid from Cuba."

[2] "Papa Joe" Cambria, the Washington scout who discovered Zoilo. Joe's advice: "Eat, sleep and think baseball."

[3] Boyhood hero: Zoilo patterned himself after Willie Miranda, a star shortstop in Cuba and later a major leaguer—a man whom Casey Stengel, pictured with him here, called a sensational fielder.

[4] Playing in the big leagues was not as easy as it looked.
In his first major league game, against the White Sox, Zoilo misses a Nellie Fox pop foul.

[5] Cookie Lavagetto, manager of the Washington Senators, had a simple formula for success: "Tighter pitching and a healthy Zoilo Versalles at short."

[6] *In the second series of the 1961 season, Zoilo so unnerves Oriole Jim Gentile with baserunning like this, that he eventually causes the big first baseman to miss a grounder, allowing Zoilo to score.*

[7] *The pro's way of summing up Zoilo's hitting skill: "Quick wrists and exceptional power for his size."*

8] On June 23, 1961, Zoilo learns that his team will have a new manager. Owner Calvin Griffith (center) announces that Sam Mele (left) will replace Cookie Lavagetto (right).

9] "A player with a great feeling for the game, a powerful arm, sure hands, and excellent speed." Here Zoilo helps complete a double play against the Yankees.

[10] Zoilo, starting shortstop for the 1963 American League all-star team, backs up a throw that gets away from Yankee Bobby Richardson.

[11] Opening day at Metropolitan Stadium in 1964: Zoilo steals second and a moment later scores as the Twins beat the Senators, 7–6.

[12]   1964 Rookie of the Year
Tony Oliva,
*author of the famous statement
"beisbol, she is all I know,"
shouts encouragement to
his friend Zoilo.*

[13]   Coach Billy Martin (center)
*talks over pre-season strategy
with American League President
Joe Cronin (left) and Sam Mele.
Martin promises to make Zoilo
"the most valuable player
in the American League."*

[14] *Led by an inspired Zoilo Versalles, the Twins blaze through their opening games of 1965. Zoilo keeps the opposition off guard by mixing power with finesse: Here he lays down a perfect bunt.*

[15] Only points out of first place in the American League, the Twins roar into Yankee Stadium on June 20th. After losing the first two games, they play a Sunday doubleheader before 71,245 fans, the largest American League crowd in ten years, and win both games.

[16] *Playing an exciting brand of baseball, Zoilo puts the Twins on top to stay as they head into the pennant stretch. Here he scores the tying run in the ninth against the Angels.*

[17] *The Versalles family, left to right: Zoilo, Luz Maria, Ester, Amparito, Angella and Maria Josefa.*

[18] *Collision at second base: Zoilo and Fred Valentine crash into each other when the Washington outfielder attempts a steal. Valentine gets up. Zoilo doesn't. The loss of Minnesota's star shortstop might have cost them the pennant, but the rugged Zoilo returns to the lineup two days later.*

[19]. *In the pennant-clinching game, Catcher Earl Battey guards the plate as Don Zimmer scores Washington's lone run, not enough to offset Zoilo's two. The Twins become the 1965 American League champions.*

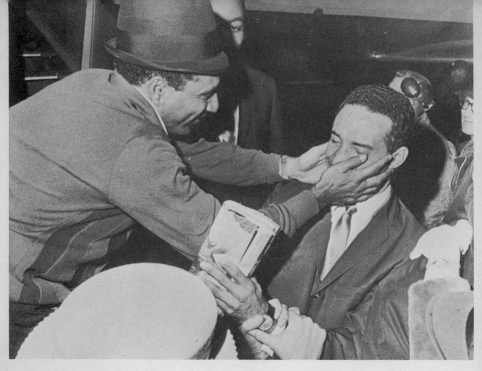

[20] Zoilo and the Twins return to Minnesota after winning the pennant.
*The shortstop is greeted warmly by his brother Lazaro and other delirious
Minnesota fans.*

[21] A proud moment: Zoilo stands with his father prior to the opening
World Series game.

[22] *Zoilo leads the Twins' power attack against Don Drysdale and the Dodgers by blasting a three-run homer in the first game of the Series.*

[23] *Zoilo dishes out some of the Dodgers' own medicine: heads-up baserunning. The Twins take the first game, 8–2.*

[24] *In the second game Zoilo's boldness upsets relief pitcher Ron Pe*ranowski, *who wild-pitches Zoilo home.*

[25] *Back at Dodger Stadium, not even such heroic efforts as Zoilo's di*for a Ron Fairly smash can save the Twins from three straight defeats.*

[26] *Die-hard Minnesota fans break down a wire fence to shake hands with Zoilo on his return from Los Angeles. Their enthusiasm spurs the Twins to a sixth-game World Series victory.*

[27] *Zoilo seemingly steals an all-important base in the final game of the Series, but is forced to return to first when the homeplate umpire rules "batter's interference."*

[28] The ball "had double stamped" all over it,
a true Versalles smash."
But Jim Gilliam makes the incredible play that takes the World Series away from Zoilo and the Minnesota Twins.

[29] The Minnesota Twins—1965 American League Champions. Top row, left to right: Jerry Zimmerman, Frank Quilici, Camilio Pasqual, Bill Pleis, Rich Rollins, Earl Battey, Zoilo Versalles, Joe Nossek, Jimmie Hall, Harmon Killebrew, Tony Oliva. Middle row: Jerry Kindall, Dave Boswell, Jim Merritt, Andy Kosco, Jim Kaat, Don Mincher, Dick Stigman, Jim Perry, Jim Grant, Al Worthington. First row: Ray Crump, Sandy Valdespino, Bob Allison, Mel Nelson, John Sain, Hal Naragon, Sam Mele, Jim Limon, Billy Martin, Johnny Klippstein, John Sevcik, Doc Lentz. Seated in front: Batboys John Natwick, Mark Stodghill, Dennis King.

she needed now was a plane seat, and she would be on her way.

Zoilo grinned. "Then I move, you bet. I chase the Red Sox clear out of Metropolitan Stadium!" And that's exactly what he and his teammates did, as they took both ends of a double-header, 6–5 and 6–3. Zoilo drove in the winning run in the opening game and scored twice in the second one. He also played a great game at short stop.

There was no keeping him down the rest of the week. When the White Sox came to Bloomington on July 3, Zoilo led the Twins to a 7–6 victory. He scored the tying run in the sixth and drove across the winning run in the eighth. Next day, July 4, before a crowd of over thirty thousand home town fans, the Twins swept another double bill. This time they beat a surprised Chicago ball club, 6–4 and 4–2, with Zoilo hitting a big triple and a pair of doubles.

He breezed into the locker room after the twin victory, his dark face beaming. He was now playing at top form. The team seemed to have straightened out, too. Best of all, Maria would soon be with him! He rushed through his shower and was on the way to the team bus, when manager Mele approached him. His face was sad. But then, Mele's face was always sad. "The top man wants to see you, kid. In his private office."

"Maria! He has word from my Maria!" Zoilo dashed

up the stairs, not even waiting for the elevator to take him to Cal Griffith's office.

Word had come from Maria, all right. But it was all bad. "She won't be able to join you this season, Zoilo," the club owner informed him. "I'm very sorry, but it is next to impossible to deal with the Castro government. However, we are going to keep trying—"

Zoilo was close to tears. "Without Maria, I don't play! Not here, no more! I want to go back to my own country—"

"If you do, you may never get out again."

"*Maria* may never get out! I want to be with her, with my father, with my brother!"

Cal Griffith let him talk it out. The boy was upset, and there was no reasoning with him at this point. "My mother, she don't want me to leave Cuba two years ago," Zoilo continued, struggling with his English. "I tell her I earn good money playing baseball in the United States. But she die. What good is money if I don't see her again? Now, my wife, she not here. I go home!"

Cal Griffith took a long breath. "I understand your feelings, Zoilo. But don't do anything foolish. Go to the hotel and sleep on it, promise me that."

"I go, but I don't sleep!"

After he left, Griffith reached for the telephone. His face was set. "Operator, get me long distance. Havana,

Cuba. I want to put in a call to the American Embassy there, and I don't care if it takes all night."

Zoilo Versalles went to his hotel room and shut himself in. Even roommate Sandy Valdespino had trouble getting in.

"Man, play it cool," Sandy advised. "The boss man is doing all he can."

Zoilo heard nothing. He turned his face to the wall. He lay there all night without even taking off his clothes. Maria couldn't come to him, and he couldn't go to Maria. The fact was, Zoilo had no money, and the club secretary had been instructed not to advance him his salary until further notice.

"Then I stay right here in the hotel," he told Sandy next morning. "I stay here until I see my wife, or until they send me home." Nothing mattered to him now, not even his career. So Zoilo took off his clothes and crawled into bed.

Zoilo refused to go out to the ball park next day. Without him the Twins lost, 6–2. He remained in his room, hopeful that Cal Griffith might change his mind about sending him home.

The phone rang just before game time. The club was flying to Washington, D.C., for the next game, and it was Sam Mele, hot under the collar. "If you are not on that plane tonight, Zoilo, I'm going to suspend you and fine you five hundred dollars!"

"I stay here," Zoilo insisted, "until Maria Josefa come here or I go to her." He couldn't stand being separated from her any longer.

When he failed to show up on the Twins' private plane, the management released the news that Zoilo was fined and suspended. But to Zoilo, it made little difference. The way he felt, baseball was a thing of the past.

Many Minnesota fans rushed to his defense. One letter, printed in a local paper, pretty much summed up public opinion on him. "You take a poor, scared young kid," the fan wrote, "sign him for next to nothing, and when he does become a major league player, you pay him the lowest salary possible. Here you have one of the greatest short stop prospects in many years, and you treat him like he is Castro's favorite boy. I think Zoilo has reason to complain!"

Another newspaper dubbed him the "Lonesome Latin." Letters of sympathy, offers of help, poured in from loyal fans. But Zoilo refused to give in. And so he continued to be kept off the team. Meanwhile the Twins floundered, losing more games than they won.

But then, on the morning of July 15, 1961, just when everything seemed darkest for the "Lonesome Latin," he received a phone call from Cal Griffith.

"Get ready to hop a plane to Miami, Zoilo. We just

got word that your wife is scheduled to leave Cuba at noon today."

Zoilo shook his head at the telephone. "I don't believe—" He couldn't help but think that this would be another false alarm. He couldn't bear to go through that kind of disappointment again.

"It is true," the owner's voice shot back. "She's coming in under a special rule. Just a minute—" He switched telephones. "Go ahead, Havana!"

"Zoilo?" asked a young woman's voice.

"Maria!" Zoilo almost jumped out of his shoes. "Is it you, truly?"

"Truly, Zoilo!" Maria's voice was faint, but clear. "I am at the Havana air field. My aunt and I, we leave at noon, Cuban time."

"*Señor* Griffith," Zoilo was already packing a bag with his free hand, "you are the greatest man in all of America!"

Mr. and Mrs. Zoilo Versalles met again in Miami on July 15, 1961, with a battery of press cameras looking on. "Lonesome Latin Lonesome No More," one newspaper announced.

Zoilo was delighted. Now he was ready to play baseball again—and good baseball, too.

In Los Angeles, where the Twins were dropping a 4–1

decision to the Angels, Sam Mele heard the news with a deep feeling of relief.

And back in Minneapolis, where Doctor Proffitt examined the results of Zoilo's blood tests, the team physician made his report. "Versalles has been suffering from poisoning due to worms. The condition probably dates back to his poor diet as a child. The wonder of it is that he has been able to play this long."

To Sam Mele, when he returned, the doctor said, "With my medicine and Maria's cooking, I think we will see a new Zoilo out at short stop."

"Just make him the old one, and I will be satisfied," the manager grunted.

Zoilo returned to the line-up on July 25. His teammates greeted him in the locker room by crossing bats over his head, as in a mock wedding procession. Somebody brought in a bag of rice and threw it at him. Somebody else sang the "Wedding March." Everyone was feeling good. The players knew they needed the kid from Cuba at short just as much as he needed them.

When Zoilo scampered out to his position that night, the home crowd cheered him loudly. He tipped his cap, then waved to a field box where Maria was sitting. To Zoilo, she looked as if she were the happiest woman in the ball park.

The Twins, who were playing the Washington Senators that night, battled down to the wire. The score was

78

2–1 in favor of the Senators when Zoilo came up to bat in the seventh inning. With the count one ball and one strike on him, he swung at an inside pitch and sent it screaming down the left field foul line. It was fair by a foot. He steamed into second and then, seeing the outfielder still bending down over the ball, he headed for third. But the throw from left field came in strong and true. Zoilo slid right into the ball.

"Out!" the umpire waved.

The Twins lost 2–1. Still, they looked like a different team with Versalles back at short.

They played like a different team, too, for the rest of the home stand, ripping off five victories in a row.

The second half of the season was the same as the beginning for Zoilo. He had to play himself into shape all over again. By the middle of August, he had gained back his batting eye and his average was climbing close to .300. The Twins were playing thrilling ball, and the fans turned out by the thousands.

Zoilo played with an ease that was a pleasure to watch. No one seeing him at short would have believed that a month before he had been the problem child of the Twins. Where ever he and Maria went, they were greeted warmly by friends and strangers alike. Zoilo had found a home.

"His attitude," Sam Mele told newspaper men, "has improved one hundred per cent. He's having more fun."

The Twins' September drive raised them to seventh place, not too bad for a team that had been in or close to the cellar since the first month of the campaign. In his first full year of major league baseball, Zoilo ran up a fine record, in spite of his trouble in the middle of summer. Playing in 129 games, he came to bat 510 times and got 143 hits, including twenty-five doubles, five triples, and seven home runs. He ended the season with a batting average of .280. The word around the league was that the kid from Cuba was going to be a real star.

On the day the season ended, Cal Griffith held a news conference and announced, "Mele is going to be our manager for 1962. He has shown me he has what it takes to lead the team."

Zoilo Versalles also had something to say to the news men. "My wife and I, we buy a house in Bloomington this winter," he told them. "Not go back to Cuba. My home is now here, in America." The news men scribbled it all down. When Maria poked him gently in the ribs, Zoilo broke out into a smile, his even teeth showing white against his dark skin.

"Oh, sí. My wife also say we stay here so our children be good Americans. Maria, she expect her first baby next April!"

CHAPTER 7

Seasons in the Sun

The beginning of the 1962 season was an important time for Zoilo in many ways.

First, he had signed a new contract at twice his first year's salary. After only one full season in the majors, he was already being compared by some to two fine American League short stops, Tony Kubek of the Yankees and Luis Aparicio of the White Sox.

"I'm nowhere near them in money," he told his wife. "But some day I get there."

Second, Zoilo had new responsibilities—he was now a father. Maria had given birth to a beautiful little girl named Amparito—little Amparo, named after his mother. The baby was born just three days before the 1962 season opened.

The Versalles family now had a home of its own in Bloomington, just a short drive from Metropolitan Stadium. A modern ranch house, it was large enough to hold Maria's aunt and Zoilo's brother Lazaro, who had also managed to leave Cuba during the previous winter. Zoilo took great pride in his new home. It was a far cry from the one-room hut in which he had been born just a little more than twenty-one years before.

Now, too, he was in the best of health. When asked about his physical condition that spring, the new father smacked his glove to make his point. "Back, she is okay. Stomach, she is okay. Somebody better watch out!" He was full of confidence.

"How many games do you expect to play this year?" asked Ray Scott, one of the three men who broadcast the games for WCCO in Minneapolis.

The short stop thought a moment. "Oh—168."

"But there are only 162 games," Scott reminded him.

Zoilo grinned. "I count World Series games, too, you bet!"

One thing which was adding to the young man's confidence was his ability to speak better English. Although he still was bothered by the difference between Spanish and English speech sounds, he had no difficulty making himself understood by newspaper men, ball players, or fans. Besides, Zoilo had found a great new friend and helper in "Banker Bob" Erickson. Erickson, a great baseball fan who was also a Minneapolis banker, had offered to steer Zoilo through his personal banking difficulties and the problems of buying a house. "Banker Bob" became one of Zoilo's closest friends, on and off the field.

When the new season opened, the Associated Press picked the Twins to finish in seventh place. Most other experts agreed.

The young short stop felt like a veteran on opening day. On his left was Bernie Allen, a former college boy with crew-cut and strong build. On his right was Rich Rollins, another college boy. Between the two of them, they had not played more than a dozen big league games. Vic Power, a good fielder, was on first. Vic, who also played the outfield, had been gained in a spring trade with the Cleveland Indians. He was exchanged for first-line pitcher Pedro Ramos.

In another change, Billy Martin had been released and made a scout. "Glad we kept Billy in the organization," Mele told Griffith. "Never know when you are going to need an old hand like that."

The Twins lost the 1962 opening game to Kansas City, although the young infielders played well. The team, then, lost four more in a row, making the experts who had picked them to finish seventh look good.

But then the Twins' big bats began to boom. Killebrew, Allison, and Earl Battey got the range, and the team started to move. By the middle of May, Minnesota was in second place with twenty games won and thirteen lost. The reasons for their success were obvious. Bernie

Allen had hit in eleven straight games, Rich Rollins was batting .350, and Zoilo had already hit five home runs.

Zoilo was also running better than ever. In one game against the Yankees, the Twins went into the thirteenth inning tied, 2–2. With one out and Bob Allison on second, Zoilo came to bat. As he stepped to the plate, the lights in the stadium were beginning to cut through the late Sunday gloom.

"Let's go!" Bernie Allen called out from the batter's circle. "We've got a plane to catch."

Versalles nodded, drawing his bat back. On the next pitch, he snapped his wrists and got good wood on the ball. *Bing!* A line single shot out to center, scoring Allison from second.

Up came Allen and bunted Zoilo to second. With only one away, manager Mele sent in John Goryl to pinch hit for the Twins' pitcher. John hit a slow grounder to the right of the mound. Zoilo, with a burst of speed, was almost to third before the pitcher picked up the ball and threw out the runner at first. But Versalles never stopped. He rounded third and lit out for home. The huge Yankee crowd roared in alarm. Joe Pepitone threw the ball to catcher Elston Howard—but too late. Zoilo slid across the plate for a commanding two-run lead. The Twins won, 4–2.

Though Zoilo ran and fielded well, except for a wild

throw now and then, as the season went on his hitting tailed off to a mere .215. "Something, she is wrong," he muttered, as he struck out twice in a row against the speed ball of Dean Chance of the Angels. He touched his temples. "Like too many baseballs in front of eyes, boss," he told Mele. "Only I don't hit any of them."

"You probably need glasses," Mele answered. "Better get your eyes checked."

Zoilo was given a brief rest on the bench, while Orlando Martinez took over at short. With drops in his eyes Versalles couldn't play, anyway.

Three days later Zoilo returned to the line-up, sporting a pair of lightly tinted glasses. "Oh, I see good now," he grinned. "I look smarter, too, no?"

He began to hit smarter immediately. He got two sharp singles that day, and another pair of hits the next day. His fielding, always good, actually improved when he began wearing glasses. He played perfect ball for the next twenty-nine days.

By July 4, 1962, the middle point of the season, the Twins were in second place, which delighted Minnesota fans and puzzled everyone else. Zoilo, however, was again having batting trouble. He was meeting the ball well, but his hits weren't "dropping in." Instead, they were going right to the fielders. His average fell to .203.

"Bench him?" Mele said when the idea of pulling

Zoilo out of the line-up was suggested. "Not while we are winning. Sure, the kid isn't getting his hits, but he's moving all the way." As if to prove his point, the infield clicked off eleven double plays in a four-game stand against Cleveland, and Zoilo was a part of every one.

The team as a whole played .600 ball for July and most of August. Usually that is good enough to stay at or close to the top.

But the first-place Yankees that year weren't a usual team—they were a great team. Led by Mickey Mantle, Roger Maris, Joe Pepitone, and Elston Howard, all of whom were hitting the long ball, they rolled up twenty-three wins in July. And they lost only eight for a near .750 average. They were five games ahead of the second-place Twins.

Zoilo, meanwhile, began to pull out of his hitting trouble. It was only a matter of time before his batted balls began to grow "eyes"—that is, before they began to squirt past the infielders' gloves for base hits. Better still, Zoilo began to hit the long ball again. On Sunday, August 19, he powered his fifteenth home run of the season in a sweep of the Red Sox. It was a famous blast for him and for the club.

"And with that home run," Herb Carneal of radio station WCCO told his audience, "Zoilo Versalles has just established a new record for club short stops. The old team record, fourteen, was set in 1930 by Joe

86

Cronin, great Senator short stop of the past, and now president of the American League. Wait a minute—! I see that one of the umpires is motioning to the fan who caught that home run ball—and yes, the fan is throwing it down on the field so that it can be presented to Zoilo Versalles. Couldn't happen to a nicer guy!"

Zoilo took good care of that ball. It was important to him. It meant that in his second year in the major leagues, he had hit more home runs in one season than any other short stop in Twins-Senators history—as far back as 1901, when the American League was founded.

As August came to a close, the Twins made their run at the Yankees, who were leading the league. The Minnesota club was given a big lift by Jack Kralick's no-hit, no-run game on Sunday, August 26, against the Kansas City A's. On August 29, they won their third straight with a 2–0 victory over the White Sox. Zoilo drove in both runs with a line smash. He also started three double plays and handled ten chances without error.

But a winning charge by the Yankees, and a three-game loss by the Twins after Labor Day, all but put their title hopes out of reach. What looked like the finish was a one-hit, 5–0 loss, to pitcher Dean Chance of the Angels, with the only safety being made by Versalles.

"That Chance, he's one tough *hombre*," Zoilo muttered. "Some day he's going to win thirty games a year. Hope they are all against the Yankees!"

The September stretch was marked by the arrival of a new team member—a tall, thin, rookie from Cuba. "Boys, meet Tony Oliva," Sam Mele introduced the new man to the team. "Zoilo, show him around, will you? They tell me his English is worse than yours was when you first came up."

"*Buenos días!*" the short stop greeted Oliva. Then they were off in a flood of Spanish, which included an invitation to dinner from Zoilo. Zoilo knew well what it meant to get a home-cooked native meal.

That September of 1962 Tony Oliva was the rawest of rookies. He had had only one season in the minors. Yet it was obvious to anyone who knew anything about baseball that the tall outfielder was a hard hitter. However, like most rookies, he was clumsy in the field and somewhat confused on the bases.

"You will learn," Zoilo told him. "If I could do it, Tony, you can, too. With a great talent like yours, it will only take time and patience." Although both were the same age, Zoilo could not help but feel like an older brother to Oliva.

With one friend found, Zoilo lost another. Much to his sorrow, word came from Cuba that Papa Joe Cambria, the kindly scout who had discovered so many Latin American stars, had died at the age of seventy-two.

"I owe that man everything," Zoilo told Tony, who

was now his roommate on the road. "If not for him, I would still be playing in the Cuban bush leagues."

Oliva nodded. He, too, had been discovered by Papa Joe. But in September, 1962, he was still a long way from having arrived as a ball player.

The Twins closed out the 1962 season with ninety-one wins and seventy-one losses for a second-place finish. They were right behind the pennant-winning Yankees. It was a far better showing than anyone had expected. Their fans ran up a record home attendance of almost 1,500,000, second only to the Yankees, whose ball park had nearly twice as many seats as Metropolitan Stadium.

Stars filled the Twins line-up. Sam Mele placed right behind Bill Rigney of the third-place Angels as the American League's Manager-of-the-Year. Pitcher Camilo Pascual won twenty games. Harmon Killebrew hit forty-eight home runs, most in the league that year. And Zoilo Versalles became the first short stop in the history of baseball to play 160 games!

He also ran up a new 1962 mark for American League infielders, by handling 501 assists. And he had a part in more double plays—127—than any other infielder, except first basemen. Best of all, he led his team in fielding with a .970 mark and made only twenty-six errors, a great improvement for him over past seasons. While his batting average dropped to .241, his slugging average remained high. He knocked in sixty-seven runs to lead all other short stops in the league.

At the usual year-end dinner, baseball writers, men from radio station WCCO, local officials, and fans honored the Twins' team members for their great performances. When it came to Zoilo's turn, "Banker Bob" Erickson hailed him as "a player with a great feeling for the game, a powerful arm, sure hands, and excellent speed."

The 1963 season was practically a mirror image of the 1962 campaign for Zoilo and the Twins. The team finished strongly in third place, behind the champion New York Yankees, and the Chicago White Sox. Camilo Pascual again was a twenty-game winner—this time with twenty-one victories. And "Killer" Killebrew led the American League once more with forty-five home runs. The team's at home attendance was also good, this time topping the previous year's mark.

As for Zoilo, he had the finest all-around season in his major league career, and was selected to start at short for the American League in the All-Star game, played in Cleveland that summer. "It is a great honor," he said with sincerity. And it was—Zoilo Versalles that day took the field with such baseball greats as Sandy Koufax, Maury Wills, Willy Mays, Mickey Mantle, and Hank

Aaron. He singled in his only official time at bat, as the National League topped the American League, 5–3.

There were other things about the two seasons that were similar, also. Zoilo became a father for the second time, when his wife gave birth to another daughter, Esthersita.

Tony Oliva, who had been sent back to the minors for more training at the start of the campaign, joined the club again at the tail end of the season. Tony's English had improved somewhat, but not as much as his batting. "You are on the team next year for certain, Tony," Zoilo encouraged him.

The year before, only Minnesota fans had honored Zoilo, but as the 1963 season drew to a close, *Look* magazine decided to pay tribute to the young Cuban. The magazine named him the top American League short stop of the year. And with good reason. Zoilo wound up the season with a .261 batting average. That included thirty-one doubles and thirteen triples—to lead the league in that department—and ten home runs.

No question about it now—Zoilo Versalles had arrived as a major league star. And to prove it, held out for, and received, a 1964 contract for a major league salary of $25,000 a year.

Not bad for the former kid from Cuba who, only eight years before, was thrilled to get forty cents bus fare after his first baseball try out!

CHAPTER 8

Two Kids from Cuba

An air of excitement, like the spring sunshine itself, poured over the Twins' training camp in March, 1964.

The club now had a seasoned manager in Mele, the league's leading home-run hitter in Killebrew, the circuit's strike out king in Pascual, two great young outfielders in Jimmy Hall and Bob Allison, a fine rookie prospect in Tony Oliva, and the league's All-Star short stop in Zoilo Versalles. They were loaded.

"We are thinking pennant," Mele told news men.

Many of them agreed. The Twins had a lot of support in 1964, enough to be named second to the Yankees in most pre-season polls.

As for local fans, they expected great things. "How can we miss?" they asked one another.

Zoilo himself was in top shape, weighing a solid 155 pounds as the team broke training camp. For the first time during his entire four years in the majors, he felt secure. He really felt like a professional. He was making good money, his family was happy and growing, and he owned a comfortable home in Minnesota. He liked it there, and Minnesota people seemed to like having him. The previous winter he had served as a public relations man for the club and traveled all over the Upper Middle West, making new friends for the Twins. Everything seemed to be going great.

The team opened the 1964 campaign on the road, winning four out of the first six games. Zoilo was hitting a strong .320 and Tony Oliva an even stronger .394.

"They are too good to be true," Sam Mele smiled happily. "Now I've got *two* kids from Cuba!"

The Twins came home to Metropolitan Stadium on April 22, determined to give local fans their first home opening game victory since moving to Minnesota. For a while, however, it looked like the old opening day story, as the Washington Senators scored four times in the top half of the first.

But Tony Oliva started the comeback, by slamming out a two-run homer his first time at bat. The Twins scored three more times later in the game, thanks to some heavy hitting by Killebrew. By the fifth inning they had taken a narrow 5–4 lead.

Up came Zoilo in the bottom of the sixth. He beat out an infield hit for his second safety of the day, and raced to second a moment later with a clean steal. He scored when relief pitcher Jim Perry hit a surprise single to center. Now it was 6–4 in favor of the Twins. However, the Senators were far from whipped. They tied the score in their half of the ninth, as a chill wind blew in from the north.

Zoilo, teeth chattering from the cold, led off the home half with a walk. When the next two players failed to advance him, it looked as though the game would drag on into extra innings. Then Bob Allison hit a single to left, sending Versalles scampering to third.

Battey was the next batter. He took a strike, then fouled off the second pitch. Zoilo edged off third, making several false starts toward home. This bothered the catcher so much that he let the next pitch, a low outside curve, roll off his glove for a short passed ball.

"Go!" the third base coach screamed. But Zoilo never heard him—he was already half way home. He slid across with the winning run that sent everyone except the Senators out of the ball park in a happy frame of mind. The Twins had won their first opening game at home, and the victory was largely due to Zoilo's great base running.

Yet not all of the little short stop's speed, or Oliva's hitting, or the home runs by Killebrew, Allison, and Hall could lift the team much over the .500 mark during the first month of play. On May 3, for example, the Twins hit seven home runs against Kansas City, but dropped both games by scores of 7–4 and 8–7.

"The home-run-or-nothing Twins," sports writers were beginning to call them.

"The worst mound staff in the league," fans added.

The club plowed through May and June, knocking down fences. But poor pitching kept them in fourth place, in spite of Zoilo's sparkling play and Oliva's fine hitting. The batting averages for both men stayed around the .400 mark for the first two months.

A strong friendship developed between the two young Cubans. They were always together on the road. "Best roommate I ever had," Versalles said of Oliva. "He doesn't smoke, doesn't drink, and doesn't snore. All he does is eat, sleep, and breathe baseball."

When told of Zoilo's remarks, the big outfielder grinned. "*Sí,*" he agreed, "*beisbol,* she is all I know."

As the season progressed, Zoilo began to get on base so often that Sam Mele moved him up from the seventh spot to the lead-off post. This suited him just fine. When ever he got on base now, he was in a perfect position to be driven home by Oliva, who batted third.

And that's just the way it worked, time after time. Zoilo would walk, or rap out a single, or get hit by a pitch. Then, Tony would step up to the plate and send him around. It happened often enough to make the combination a real scoring threat.

The Minnesota pitching, however, stumbled along. In June, the Twins lost three straight to Detroit, 10–5, 16–1, and 5–4. Other games went 8–7, 13–2, and 8–1 against them. Relief pitchers Bill Pleis and Johnny Klippstein became arm weary. When starting pitchers Pascual, Kaat, and Perry finally did give a good pitching performance, the hitters failed to come through. The result was a series of heart-breaking losses by scores of 3–2, 2–1, and 2–0.

But Zoilo refused to quit. He had one of his best nights at bat on June 4, as the home team swamped the Baltimore Orioles, 11–5, in a slam, bang affair. Such games were becoming the usual thing for the Twins. Versalles went four-for-five in that game—four hits in five times at bat. The total included two home runs and a pair of singles.

After the game, one of the news men asked Mele what would happen if his short stop ever got hurt. "Don't ask!" the manager exclaimed.

The next week, however, the Twins made a big trade, sending outfielders Lenny Green and Vic Power to the Angels for infielder Jerry Kindall. Kindall was to be a back-up man for both Versalles at short stop and Bernie Allen at second, where ever the need developed. Zoilo responded with another big night as he went four-for-four—a double, a triple, and two smashing singles—to lead the Twins to a 5–3 win over the Senators.

The trade with the Angels was made just in time. On June 13, Bernie Allen, going back for a pop fly, turned, tripped, and fell, his leg twisting under him. "He will be out for a month," Doctor Proffitt said after examining the young second baseman. So Versalles had a new partner at second, Jerry Kindall.

Two days later the Twins made another major trade, getting pitcher Jim "Mudcat" Grant from Cleveland for lefty Lee Stange. This would prove to be one of the best deals Cal Griffith ever made.

As the 1964 All-Star game approached, it looked as though the Minnesota Twins had taken over the entire American League line-up. Tony Oliva, still batting over .330, was named to right field. Harmon Killebrew, with twenty home runs to his credit, was named to left. And Bob Allison, who had been shifted to first, won the starting post at that position. Zoilo, too, was in the running again, but this time he was nosed out by rookie Jim Fregosi. Fregosi had been playing great ball for the Angels.

"That's all right," Zoilo told news men who questioned him about the choice. "The best man won out."

Sam Mele nodded in satisfaction. A year before, Zoilo might not have taken the decision quite so easily.

Actually, now, Versalles welcomed the three day break.

It gave him a chance for a much needed rest and a few days at home with Maria, who was expecting again. Soon afterward, on August 4, she gave birth to another girl, their third.

"We call her Angela," Zoilo said happily. "She looks just like her mother, an angel."

Zoilo was also busy that summer trying to get his father out of Cuba. The older Versalles had been hoping to join his son in America for almost two years, but had not been able to leave the country. Still, Zoilo knew he had to keep his mind on business—baseball business. That way he would be in the best possible position to help his father when the time came.

After the All-Star break, it was back to baseball for Zoilo and the Twins. And one of the worst nose dives in the Twins' short history followed. They lost seventeen games, while winning only seven during the rest of July. Zoilo played his heart out in that stretch, but the Twins' big bats were strangely silent.

Still, Versalles never let up. Usually he would have brooded after a defeat. Now he was the first to talk it up. "All right, if you big guys don't hit, we little fellows will have to do it," he chirped, as the Twins flew into Chicago after losing their eighth straight. That night he proved that he meant what he said. The White Sox were battling the Yankees and the Orioles for first place, but Zoilo managed to hit two home runs, driving in four runs, and giving his team a 6–3 win.

The following week, after losing four straight, Zoilo

broke the string again with a pair of home runs against the Orioles, for a 7–4 victory.

August was a little better. Oliva and Killebrew began to find the range. With newly acquired Red Worthington giving some much needed late inning mound help, the club managed to win more games than it lost that month. They wound up August with a .500 record—sixty-six won, sixty-six lost—and September was still ahead.

Sam Mele urged a final effort. He wanted to finish in the first division. "Remember the World Series checks, boys," he told them.

But nineteen of the Twins' next thirty games were against first division clubs—New York, Chicago, Baltimore, Detroit, and Los Angeles. The "ins" did not intend to make room for the "outs." They beat down the Twins, and the Minnesota ball club ended the season under the .500 mark, in a sixth-place tie with Cleveland.

Zoilo took the end-of-season defeats hard. "We start with so much, we end with so little. I don't like to lose, not this way."

Yet he had no need to be ashamed. His own 1964 record fairly sparkled. During the season, he had played in 160 games, come to bat 659 times, and banged out 171 hits for a .259 average. Credited to him were thirty-three doubles, ten triples, and twenty home runs, breaking his own club record for home runs hit by short stops. Also, he had become one of the strongest players in baseball, having missed only eight games in three seasons of play.

"But one thing I am proud for," he confessed to news men after the season, "my roommate, Tony. Maybe he don't say much, but he sure hit a lot, *that* kid from Cuba!"

Tony Oliva certainly had, in his first season in the majors. He finished with a .323 mark, good enough to win the American League batting title.

And good enough to be named the league's Rookie of the Year for 1964.

CHAPTER 9

The
Three-hundred Dollar Shower

Zoilo Versalles spent the fall and winter of 1964–65 making personal appearances for the Twins all over Minnesota. He went from one dinner to another, talking before groups of eager fans, and he made a big hit everywhere.

However, the dinner circuit took its toll. By the time spring training rolled around, Zoilo was ten pounds over weight. George "Doc" Lentz, the team trainer, whistled up a storm when the short stop stepped on the scales. "Into the rubber suit for you, tubby! What kind of a diet have you been on?"

Zoilo patted his stomach. "Okay, Doc, I run it off!"

That fitted in well with manager Mele's plans. "We've got to get some speed in this club," he told his players before spring training started. "We need more speed to go along with our power. After each man takes batting practice, I want him to run to first. On the next batted ball, I want him to break for third and slide in. I don't care where the ball is hit. Then I want him to run into the dug out. I want every man to run, run, run—until it becomes second nature!"

Mele had come to Orlando with his mind made up to change the Twins into speed merchants. The past fall he had seen the St. Louis Cardinals whip the mighty Yankees in the World Series on speed alone. The Cardinals had really run the American League champions out of the ball park, taking the extra base and forcing the once proud Yankees into throwing errors.

To put "Operation Speed" into practice, Mele had hired Billy Martin as a coach during the previous winter. The thirty-seven-year-old former second baseman was ideal for the job. "Baseball," Billy reminded the team, "is still a game of running, throwing, and hitting. All three put together, not just one or two of the three. And it is a game of talk. You, Zoilo, let's hear you talk it up!"

Zoilo talked it up. He had done a little yelling the season before, but he was never much on it. Now he forced himself. He would call out something, anything —to the pitcher, to the catcher, to which ever teammate caught his fancy at the moment.

"Hubba-hubba-hubba-*cat!*" he called out to pitchers

Jim Kaat and "Mudcat" Grant. It was "hubba-hubba-*hoy!*" to catcher Earl Battey, "hubba-Bernie-*boy!*" to Bernie Allen at second. Soon, the other players followed his lead, and the Twins infield rapidly became known as the noisiest in the circuit. Billy Martin smiled. This was the way to talk it up!

Zoilo also ran. He ran around the bases, around the outfield, to his position, to the dug out. He ran until his tongue hung out. Little by little, the winter fat began to melt off, and before long he was his old self again. He was so fast that Billy Martin called him "Zippy Zee."

The short stop liked his new coach and did everything Billy asked him to do. Martin knew all the problems an infielder had to face on and off the field, and Zoilo appreciated this. He was the pupil, and Martin the teacher, and it was fine with him. A ball player, he reminded himself, never stops learning.

Zoilo felt Billy's eyes on him both at the plate and in the field. Yet he didn't mind, for Martin never chewed him out in public or "put him on" in front of the other players. If Billy had something to say to him, he took Zoilo off to one side and quietly explained to him how he might improve his baseball skills. For example, when Zoilo picked up his old habit of pegging wildly to first, Billy studied Zee's throwing pattern. Then he came up with an idea.

"Try throwing over hand instead of side arm as you

103

have been doing, Zee. I know, some short stops can do it that way. Marty Marion and Phil Rizzuto did. But that side arm motion of yours makes the ball 'sail' every so often. Give the over hand style a try."

Zee did, and the over hand method worked wonders. His throws from short to first now came straight and true. "His arm is so strong," the coach pointed out to manager Mele, "that he can take time to throw over hand and still catch the fastest runner in the business at first."

Zoilo himself was delighted at the improvement. No short stop, least of all one with pride, likes to be thought of as a scatter-arm. There had already been far too many jokes that spring about the usual Twins double play: from Allen to Versalles to the stands.

Even with the individual ball players working so hard, team improvement came more slowly. The running game proved a puzzle to such slow runners as Earl Battey and Harmon Killebrew. And Bernie Allen, who had had a knee operation during the winter, had trouble picking up the Billy Martin go-go methods.

The Twins failed to impress during this period of trial and error, and manager Mele knew it would take time to change the team's entire style of play. Others, however, were not as patient. One fan wrote that as far as the 1965 flag race went, "the Twins have less chance than a head of lettuce at a rabbit show." Even owner

Cal Griffith was heard to mutter as the team went through a poor record of practice games before the start of the regular season.

As spring training came to a close, Zoilo picked up a cold, not bad enough to keep him in bed, but bad enough to drain him of his usual energy.

"Better spend a couple of days in bed," Maria urged. As did most players' families, she and the children had come to Florida for spring training.

"Can't," Zoilo grunted. "Mele's not happy with the way things are shaping up. I've got to get out there, as long as I can walk."

It was obvious to everyone later that day that Zoilo was not his usual self. "What's the matter with him?" Mele growled in the middle of the game against the Mets. "He's playing like he's asleep!" By now, the manager was on edge. Here it was only a week before opening day, and the team still hadn't jelled into a playing unit.

Zoilo forced himself to play in spite of aching muscles. He said nothing to Mele or Martin. He didn't want to be known as a complainer.

In the sixth inning, with the Mets at bat, two out, and the bases loaded, Jim Hickman sent a slow ball to Zoilo's left. It looked like an easy out to end the inning. The runners only trotted around the bases. The pitcher stepped off the mound.

But, suddenly, the fans sitting under the warm Florida sun let out a gasp. Zoilo, making a late, lazy try for the ball, let it roll under his glove for a cheap single. Two runners crossed the plate.

Manager Mele bounded out of the dug out, his head thrust forward in anger. "Hey, Zoilo, what do you want out there, a butterfly net?"

Versalles kicked at the dirt, his face twisted into a guilty frown. He knew he should have had that roller!

Sam Mele called time, then waved his short stop out to the outfield. "Get out there and do some running! Maybe that will wake you up!" Turning to the bench he motioned to Bill Bethea, a second-string infielder. "Take his place, Bill. Let's show our *star* how to play the position!"

Zoilo bit down hard on his chewing gum. No need to talk like that in front of everybody. After all, he *was* the team's regular short stop. Zee stuffed his glove into a hip pocket and stalked out to the outfield, where he began a slow trot. His muscles ached even more. He was certain now that he had a fever.

Up in the press box above the stands, sports writers from the Twin Cities looked at one another. Easy-going Sam Mele was finally cracking the whip—about time!

After a few more lazy trots, Zoilo walked toward the bench. He certainly didn't feel sharp that day, he told himself. Maybe a good night's sleep—

Coach Billy Martin stopped him at the edge of the dug out. "Sam is right, Zee. If you don't move now, you won't move later."

The short stop nodded. "Okay, Billy. I move fast tomorrow. Only today, I don't feel so hot." All he wanted now was some medicine and a shower. He headed for the locker room.

But Mele called him back. "Not yet, Zee. Sit on the bench until the game is over!" Mele was still boiling mad at what he thought was poor play. "You might learn something!" he added.

Zoilo felt the blood rush to his face. Who did Mele think he was, some fresh rookie? "I sit on the bench for Martin," he shouted, "not for you!" Then Zoilo slammed his glove down.

"That crack," the manager snapped back, "will cost you just one hundred dollars!"

Zoilo was outraged. "Why not make it two hundred dollars?"

"Okay, two hundred dollars it is!"

"Make it three hundred dollars, why don't you?"

"You got it, Zee." Mele looked his short stop right in the eye. "You are fined three hundred dollars for talking out of turn."

The two glared at each other for another second. Then Zoilo marched to the locker room, tore off his uniform, threw it into the laundry cart, and stepped into a shower stall. Still furious, he turned on one of the faucets, and let out a howl, as a stream of cold water splashed over him. It cooled him off on the spot.

Through the spray Zoilo saw Billy Martin. Martin had followed him into the locker room. Zee knew how tough the coach could be about a stupid mistake, and he knew that he had certainly made a mistake talking back to his manager. He had the feeling just then that this shower could be the most expensive one of his young life.

"Tonto!" Zoilo called himself a fool in Spanish. By now he was far more angry at himself than at Mele. He knew Mele had every right to bench him or any other player for poor play. *"Tonto!"* he repeated.

Zoilo picked up a towel and began drying himself. He would have to say he was sorry for what he had said, first to Mele, then to Martin. That was the only way he could get back into the line-up by opening day.

The Twins broke camp two days later with the short stop still in the manager's dog house. Zoilo hadn't yet been able to apologize for his angry words. It would take time—and somebody to push him.

The push came from his brother Lazaro when the Twins returned home on April 11. "You are a big boy now," Lazaro reminded him. "You've got class at bat and in the field. Now you have to show your class off the field, too."

Zoilo let out a slow grin. "Okay, I go see Mele after lunch."

"Before lunch!"

The short stop sighed. "Like you say. Before lunch."

It was less difficult than he imagined. Mele, a sound baseball man, accepted Zoilo's words gracefully. But he also reminded Zoilo that on the field only one man ran the club. "Not the owner, not the coach, not a group of players, but the manager. That's what he gets paid for."

"Okay, boss. And I get paid for playing short stop, right?"

Mele smiled. "Right." He handed him the line-up card. "For opening day, Zee. I made it out just before you got here."

Zoilo glanced down. His name was in the lead-off spot, at short stop. His face broke into a grin. Things had gone well with Mele—still, Zoilo was not through explaining his actions.

As it turned out, telling Billy Martin that he was sorry was even easier. "Forget it, kid. Forget everything but baseball. Give it your best, and you will make me the smartest coach in the business. And by the end of the season I will make you the most valuable player in the American League." He winked at Zoilo. "Is it a deal, Zee?"

"It is a deal, you bet!" Zoilo answered happily.

Unfortunately, the opening day line-up turned out to have a couple of gloomy surprises for local fans. Earl Battey was out with a bad shoulder, and in his place was Gerald Zimmerman, second-string catcher. Jerry Kindall was in Bernie Allen's place at second base. Bernie's bad knee had failed to come around. Luckily, the rest of the team was more familiar. Rich Rollins was at third, and Tony Oliva was in right field and batting in the clean-up spot. Oliva was followed by Killer Killebrew at first base, Jimmy Hall in center field, Bob Allison in left, Zimmerman behind the plate, and Jim Kaat on the mound.

It was a team full of question marks. Could Tony Oliva continue to hit at his record-breaking pace? Would Bob Allison's back hold up? Was the pitching staff, loaded with rookies, deep enough? And most of all, how would the argument between Sam Mele and his short stop affect team spirit?

Baseball writers, even those in Minneapolis and St. Paul, gave the Twins no chance at all at the 1965 flag. The Associated Press picked them fifth, a much higher spot than they deserved in the eyes of most experts.

But Zoilo paid little attention to what the papers said. With his recent trouble behind him, he was anxious to get out there and play, to give his whole being to the game. He just wanted to "eat, sleep, and think baseball all the time," as the late Papa Joe Cambria had once said.

Opening day in Minnesota was spoiled by rain and floods, as the Minnesota River spilled over its banks. But the clouds parted long enough for the Twins to knock off the Yanks, 5–4. Then, it rained for another two days. Somehow, the Twins managed to get in three more games between showers that week, losing one and winning two. Even with the base paths made heavy with rain, it was obvious that the Twins were sticking to their plan: They were off and running, much to the delight of the fans, and to the surprise of the other teams.

"I don't care if you do get thrown out trying for the extra base," Mele urged his players. "I want you to keep running."

This suited the speedy Zoilo to a T. In a game against the Cleveland Indians, he scored all the way from first on a long single by Rich Rollins. Getting a good jump on the pitcher, Zee had second base all but stolen as Rollins connected. Rounding second, Zippy Zee headed for third. When outfielder Leon Wagner had trouble holding the ball, Zee turned on the steam and headed for home. He just beat the long throw from the outfield. The Twins won that game, 6–3.

The Twins took to the road after the first week with a record of three wins and one loss. Sports writers were impressed. "How good are the Twins? they asked manager Mele.

"The next twenty-one games will tell," he answered. "Nineteen of them will be played against clubs that finished in the first division last year. For us, it will be twenty-one or bust!"

The Twins blazed through those games as though they were on fire. They were led by a flash at short stop, who gobbled up everything hit his way, ran the bases like an escaping thief, and hit well over .350. Teammate Tony Oliva, although bothered by an injured middle finger on his right hand, hit for power. Meanwhile, the mound staff worked well. Camilo Pascual won four straight. Jim Mudcat Grant took three out of his first four decisions. Rookies Dave Boswell and Jerry Fosnow pitched good games. Of the twenty-one games the Twins wanted to take from those first division clubs, they managed to win fifteen, while losing only six. By the middle of May, the Minnesota club led the American League, shocking their opponents and silencing their critics.

Local fans could hardly believe it. The question on everyone's lips that spring was: "Are the Twins for real?"

CHAPTER 10

Winning the Pennant

The Twins certainly didn't look "for real" the following Sunday when they met the last-place Kansas City A's in a double bill. The A's had just fired manager Mel McGaha and signed Heywood Sullivan in his place, and they were playing special ball for their new field boss. They dumped the Twins twice.

"Just one of those things," Mele muttered. "They were all fired up."

But when his club flew out to Los Angeles and dropped two more to the Angels, it looked as though the Twins had shot their bolt. Still, they refused to give up, least of all Zoilo.

"We will get straightened out, once Tony starts hitting," he said. Oliva, bothered by that sore middle finger, was batting under .250. Versalles, himself, had hit in six straight games, but help was needed from the big man.

Help finally came—from "Tony O," as he was called

by his teammates. And it came in the next game against the Angels. The two teams went into extra innings, with the score tied 1–1. Zoilo, coming to bat with one out in the top of the twelfth, tried to put one over the wall on the first ball pitched to him. But he missed it completely. Then he dumped a perfect bunt along the third base line and beat it out for a single.

"Hubba-hubba-*Sandy!*" Zee yelled from first base. "Get me home!"

Sandy Valdespino's answer was a scratch single, which moved Zoilo to second. Then each advanced a base on a long fly to right by Rich Rollins. Now there were men on second and third, two out, and Tony O at bat.

No use giving a walk to a .250 batter, Angel pitcher Dean Chance seemed to be thinking. He would take care of Oliva himself.

Only it turned out to be the other way around. Oliva pasted Dean's first pitch into right field for a two-run single, scoring Versalles and Valdespino. The Twins won the ball game, 3–1.

Zoilo continued his hitting as the club came home for a brief two-game stand against the Athletics. He had a two-run hit in the first game for a 6–4 victory, and a double and triple in the second game, which the Twins dropped, 6–2. Tony Oliva failed to hit in the second game. Next the club headed east to Boston and friendly Fenway Park, with its short left field fence.

"Here's where our batting averages get fat," Zoilo said. "A sure cure for us."

He was right. The Twins beat the Red Sox twice, 17–5 and 9–7. Zippy Zee got five hits in those two games, Tony O, four. More important, Minnesota moved into first place by a slim margin over the White Sox.

The heavy hitting by the two former Cubans continued, as the Twins swept a three-game series with Washington. In the third game Zoilo came to bat in the fourth inning, with men on first and third and one out. The Washington infield moved in, expecting a squeeze bunt by the smart little short stop. Zoilo looked at third base coach Billy Martin. "You are on your own," came the sign from Martin. Zoilo picked out a fast ball and cracked it out of the park to bring in three runs. Minnesota tucked that game away, 6–0. It was Camilo Pascual's sixth win of the young season.

With that, the first-place Twins came home for Memorial Day. "What's keeping them up there?" sports writers were asking.

"Versalles," was Billy Martin's answer. "He has been carrying the team for the past month with both bat and glove."

"Just how good is he?" Max Nichols of the Minneapolis *Star* wanted to know.

"A sharp Versalles," the coach explained, "can be as great as Phil Rizzuto, Gil McDougald, or any of the fine short stops I've played with, or against, in my career. Put it this way: he has better speed than Rizzuto or Gil, he is as quick as Phil, and he hits with more power and has a stronger arm than either. In my book he's tops."

Zoilo's fine playing was never better displayed than in one 9–5 win over the Senators at home. In the fourth inning, with the Twins leading 1–0, Zoilo fumbled a hard-hit ground ball by Frank Howard. He kicked the dirt, gritted his teeth, and called out a "hubba-hubba-cat" to pitcher Jim Grant. "We get the next one!"

He did better than that. He got them all. First the short stop ranged far to his left, scooped up a hard smash, and threw out the runner. Then he went into the hole to take a base hit from the next batter. The third out he took care of all by himself, by leaping a foot off the ground to spear a line drive.

Back in the dug out Billy Martin grinned in satisfaction. In previous years Zee would have been upset after an error. Now he didn't let errors bother him. He came back to give it all he had.

Versalles was running hard, too. In the next game against the Senators, which the Twins won 9–2, Zee led off the fifth with a walk. Then he scooted around to third on a sharp single to right. He came into third standing up, and slowed down a little as he rounded the bag. When the right fielder made a lazy toss to second to hold the runner on first, Zoilo headed for home. He beat out the throw with plenty of time to spare. Playing Mele's running game, he had scored all the way from first on a single!

Up to now, it had been a five-club battle for first place. The Twins, the White Sox, the Orioles, the Tigers, and the Indians were all making their bids. The Yankees, who were usually American League champions, were stumbling along in the second division. But, suddenly, the Bombers began to make noises, winning eight of their next ten games. Worried Minnesota fans looked over their shoulders at the Yankee charge. "Here they come!" they warned each other.

For a while, things looked bad for the Twins. They dropped three out of four to the Indians and split a four-game series with the Tigers. When they went to Chicago on June 15 for an important series against the White Sox, they were half a game out of first place. At this point Sam Mele changed his line-up. He shifted Harmon Killebrew to third base, Rich Rollins to second, and put big Don Mincher on first. Zoilo, as usual, held down the short stop post.

The change seemed to help, and the Twins took two out of three from the Sox. The last game of the series, a 3–1 victory, was gained thanks to home runs by Don Mincher and Zoilo Versalles. It was Versalles' ninth home run of the year. Next stop for the Twins was New York.

"Bring on the Yankees!" Minnesota fans roared, following their team over radio and TV.

On Friday night, June 18, their roars were reduced to whispers when Mickey Mantle belted a grand slam home run in a 10–2 win against the visitors from Minnesota. The following day, there was an absolute hush in the Twin Cities as the Yankees whipped the Twins again, 5–3.

After two straight losses the Twins took the field Sunday before 71,245 New York fans, the largest major league crowd in ten years. The New Yorkers were making their move at last! The huge crowd had come to raise their heroes and bury the Twins.

A keyed-up Versalles heard the boos for the visiting team pouring down from the packed stands. A year or two ago he might have let it upset him. Now he had eyes and ears only for baseball.

Leading off the top of the first, he picked out an outside pitch and slapped it to right for a single, finally scoring on a long fly by Harmon Killebrew. Zoilo knocked in another run in the fourth with a double, and, in the sixth, he slammed a single to left to put Earl Battey in scoring position.

"My, oh, my!" Yankee broadcaster Red Barber announced. "Did you ever? I mean, did you ever see a busier little fellow than that Zoilo Versalles? He is absolutely all over the Yankees, and they know it!"

games after that, too. And they did it without help from two of their brightest stars. Zoilo couldn't hit the size of his hat during the winning streak. He went twenty-eight for nothing, while ace pitcher Pascual, who had won eight straight, sat on the sidelines with what looked like a strained muscle.

"I don't know," Zoilo grumbled, "I don't hit, and we still win. Maybe I better throw my bat away, eh, boss?"

Manager Mele smiled. "Just keep your glove working, Zee. You can snap out of it." He knew that the batting trouble was partly due to an old problem: concern for his family. This time it was the short stop's father. Mr. Versalles had finally managed to get out of Cuba, but he hadn't managed to get into the United States. He was trying to enter by way of Mexico.

"If Papa ever comes to live with us," Zoilo told his wife, "I could ask for nothing more."

Zoilo, senior, finally flew to Minneapolis in the middle of July. At the next home game, the proud father saw his son play major league baseball for the first time. Zippy Zee rose to the occasion by belting out two hits and driving in three runs in a 6–2 victory over the Boston Red Sox.

"Did your father's arrival have anything to do with getting over your batting problem?" reporters asked.

"I don't know," the happy short stop said. "But I sure slept better last night."

That was the last good night's sleep either he or his teammates got for the rest of the month. Trouble piled on trouble for the Twins. Camilo Pascual's problem was found to be a muscle knot in his shoulder. He had to have an operation. Bob Allison broke his wrist. Jim Kaat developed arm trouble. Catcher Earl Battey split a finger. Jerry Kindall pulled up lame. Bernie Allen had already been sent down to the minors to work off his stiff knee—it was still giving him trouble. And as if all this weren't enough, Sam Mele had a run-in with an umpire and was suspended for five days.

"Pressure!" The word flashed around the league. "The Twins are going to crack up!"

Pressure, maybe. But crack up, no. Crippled, tired, sometimes without a regular manager, and with Versalles in one of the worst batting slumps of his career—he was hitting only .230—the club somehow managed to stay on top. They did not "die in July." Instead, they won twenty-two games that month, and lost only seven.

"We are playing as a team," Mele explained happily, after his five days were up, and he was back with the team. "Jimmy Hall and Harmon Killebrew are carrying hot bats. Oliva is batting over .300 after his slow start. Zoilo is playing the best short stop in the field I've seen. Sure, our injuries have hurt us—but the teams we have been playing against haven't been able to hurt us." At the end of July, the Twins were still on top with a record of sixty-five wins, thirty-seven losses. Now they headed into the dog days of August.

With his father at home and Maria expecting their fourth child any day, Zoilo became the joke-cracking leader of the club. He was especially active after his big bat started to boom once again.

But all that changed on the night of August 2, when Russ Snyder of the Baltimore Orioles, legging out an infield hit, crashed into first baseman Harmon Killebrew. Zoilo heard the *thump* of bodies, as the two big ball players ran into each other on the base paths.

"Time!" the short stop screamed, rushing toward the fallen Killebrew. Killebrew lay on the ground, his left arm twisted under him.

A hush fell over the stands as the big first baseman was carried into the dug out. An hour later Doctor William Proffitt released the sad news:

"Killebrew has a badly damaged elbow. He will be out of action for at least a month, possibly for the rest of the season."

The Twins refused to buckle. Outfielder Joe Nossek and infielder Frank Quilici were brought up from the farm system, along with pitcher Jim Merritt. Bob Allison, his wrist mended, took over first base. Jim Kaat returned to the mound. "We are still in the lead," Zoilo reminded his teammates. "They have to catch us first."

The next day, after splitting a double bill with the

Senators, word reached Zoilo that his mother's brother, Uncle Ramos, had managed his release from Cuba and would be at the Minneapolis air field in a few hours. The Versalles family had a joyful meeting that night. Zoilo, his father, and his newly arrived uncle sat up late into the night, talking over old times. It was four o'clock in the morning before the party broke up.

"Plenty of time to rest," Zoilo assured his uncle. "We play a night game, so I can sleep all day."

But he hadn't counted on Maria. Two hours after his head touched the pillow, Maria shook him awake. "Get up, Zoilo," she whispered. "I think the baby is on the way."

Zippy Zee never moved faster. Throwing on a robe, he hurried his wife into the car and sped to the hospital. Then he paced the halls until the doctor came out to tell him, "A lovely baby girl, Zoilo. Mother and child are doing just fine!"

Versalles smiled happily. "We will call her Luz Maria," he announced. Then he went in to see his wife.

Zoilo brought the usual box of cigars with him to the ball park that evening. "Want to sit this one out?" Billy Martin asked. "I can fix it up with the boss if you are tired."

"Who is tired?" the short stop yawned. "I think I will go out and hit one for Luz Maria tonight!" And he did, getting his thirteenth home run of the 1965 season, as Minnesota beat the Senators, 8–5.

The crippled Twins continued to roll. They won five of their next six games after Killebrew's injury. By the middle of August, they were out in front by eight games. Pennant fever now gripped the entire Upper Middle West. "The magic number," one Minneapolis restaurant announced in its window, "is now forty-eight." This meant that any combination of forty-eight Minnesota victories—or losses by the club closest to them—would give the American League pennant to the Twins. It was far too early to be talking "magic numbers," but local fans were swept by a wave of enthusiasm seldom seen in baseball.

Zoilo, meanwhile, got his second wind. His average began to climb. He hit his twenty-eighth and twenty-ninth doubles of the year in an 8–2 victory against the Yankees. That twenty-eighth two-bagger was a surprise. It would have been a single for almost anyone other than the speedy Versalles. Yankee center fielder Mickey Mantle was just a little slow in picking up the ground ball to the outfield, and Zippy Zee was off and running, stretching the hit into a double.

"When I run to first and put my foot on the bag," he explained on a TV show after the game, "I take a look at the outfield. If the ball is still on the ground, I try for second. The outfielder has to make a perfect throw to get me."

Labor Day came and went, and still the Twins held their lead, although by then it had shrunk to five games. The other clubs, anxious to slow down the top teams, were throwing their best pitchers against Versalles, Oliva, and company. But Zoilo had raised his average to .260. Allison and Hall were hitting well. And the team was running as never before, dog-tired as they were. Best of all, Killebrew was now beginning to work out. His elbow was on the mend.

By September 10, the magic number had dropped to fifteen, after two big wins over the second place White Sox. Five days later, with a commanding ten game lead, the Twins' front office announced it would accept World Series ticket orders. The club then ripped off seven wins in a row.

Just three more victories, and the pennant would be theirs!—a double-header and a single game against the Senators. The Twins took the first game, 5–0. But the second contest nearly proved disastrous for both the club and for Zoilo Versalles. In the first inning, Washington outfielder Fred Valentine singled. On the next pitch, he headed for second. Zoilo hurried over to the bag to take the throw from the catcher. The toss was in plenty of time, but high and to the right of second. It pulled the short stop right into the path of the charging runner. Versalles and Valentine ran hard into each other.

"Safe!" the umpire called, as the ball and both players fell to the ground. Valentine got up. Zoilo did not.

The Twins poured out of the dug out. "Give him air!" a wild Mele called out. "If anything happened to my short stop now—"

Zoilo moved. He opened one eye. "Did I get him?" he murmured.

Teammates carried him into the locker room. After a few sniffs of smelling salts, the short stop shook his head. "Where is my glove? I've got to get back on the field."

Doctor Proffitt gently pushed him back on the training table. "You are not going anywhere but to the hospital, Zee. I want to take some pictures of your head and chest."

The plates showed nothing, but Zoilo's face did. A huge bump had come up near his eye, and his left shoulder and arm were also badly bruised. "Tough little fellow," trainer Lentz grunted when Zoilo went back to the dug out after the X rays had been taken. From the bench, he saw his team take the second game, 5–3. Now they were sure of at least a tie for the pennant.

"One more victory and we are in!" owner Cal Griffith crowed.

A Sherman tank couldn't have kept Versalles on the bench for the game that might prove to be the pennant clincher. "I'm okay," he assured Maria by telephone. She had seen the accident the day before on TV. "A little sore, but okay. Honest! How are the children?"

"They are all fine," she answered. "Everyone is fine. And now that we know you are fine too, all we wish is for you to win and come home safe."

Zoilo took the field on Sunday, September 26, wondering at a curious chain of events. Five years ago, the team on which he was now the star short stop had left Washington to become the Minnesota Twins. Now they were back in the nation's capital about to win their first flag—provided they could defeat the very team that had taken their place in the American League.

The Senators were well aware of the fact. They battled the visitors down to the wire, and led them 1–0 going into the top of the sixth. Kaat, the first Minnesota batter, popped up. Then Zoilo stepped to the plate, looking at the pitcher out of his sore left eye.

"Ball one!" the umpire called. A strike and a ball followed. Then Zoilo steadied his bat. There it was— the pitch he was waiting for, a fast ball on the inside corner. He whipped the bat around and sent a hard drive over third base, deep into the left field corner. By the time the ball was picked up, Zoilo was standing on third base, brushing the dust off his uniform.

Now he edged off the base. The Senator pitcher eyed

him nervously. Zoilo made a quick motion toward home as the pitcher wound up. "Hubba-hubba-*go!*" he yelled.

This time it was the Washington catcher who was upset by Zoilo's false start toward home. He looked up just long enough to take his eye off the pitch, and the ball glanced off his mitt and skidded all the way back to the backstop. Zoilo could have waltzed in with the tying run, but he didn't. Instead he dashed in and jumped on the plate with both feet.

He came to bat again in the eighth inning with the score still tied 1-all. Frank Quilici was on third with what could be the winning run. The Senator infield came in, guarding against the expected squeeze. But Zoilo, getting the hit sign from coach Billy Martin, swung away. He powered a long smash to the outfield, long enough to drive in the run that was to win both game and pennant. It was his seventy-seventh RBI of the season.

An inning later, when Zoilo Versalles made a leaping one-handed catch for the final Washington out, the Minnesota Twins stormed off the field. They were 2–1 victors, and 1965 champions of the American League!

CHAPTER 11

The Most Valuable Player

The Twins played out the season as happy as a bunch of teen-agers on a picnic. Meanwhile, a fierce dog fight had developed for the National League flag between the Los Angeles Dodgers and the San Francisco Giants.

"Doesn't make any difference which of them comes out on top," Zoilo laughed. "They still have to take the field nine men at a time, same as us."

One of the big questions that final week was who would be chosen as the American League's Most Valuable Player. The junior circuit had several good candidates: pitcher Mel Stottlemyre of the Yankees; Dick McAuliffe, Tiger short stop; Brooks Robinson of the Orioles, last year's MVP; and Carl Yastrzemski, Red Sox outfielder.

The Twins themselves had three men in the running: Tony Oliva, who was the league's batting champion for the second year in a row; Mudcat Grant, the twenty-one-game winner on the mound; and Zippy Zee himself. Sports writers around the league would select the winner and announce their choice later in the fall.

Zoilo had a fine record to support his claim as the American League's Most Valuable Player. He led the league in most total bases—301. That was more than such great hitters as Rocky Colavito of the Indians, Brooks Robinson, and teammates Oliva and Allison, truly remarkable for such a slightly built player.

Versalles also led the American League in runs scored —126—and most times at bat—660. He tied for the lead in doubles—forty-five—and triples—twelve. His batting average for 1965 was a respectable .271 in spite of the slump he had suffered in the middle of the season.

Yet he insisted the honor should go to Tony Oliva. "His hitting brought us the pennant," he said. "Tony was the most valuable to the team." The writers, however, would wait until after the World Series to make their decision known.

The Los Angeles Dodgers squeaked through to win the National League crown, led by the powerful pitching of Sandy Koufax and Don Drysdale. And sparked by the clever Maury Wills at short stop, they were solid favorites against Minnesota.

"Lucky if the Series goes to five games," experts said. "The Twins are game, but they are not in the same class as the Dodgers."

The World Series opened in Metropolitan Stadium on Wednesday, October 6. It was a bright, clear day. As Zoilo stepped out of the Twins dug out, he looked over the packed stands. Never before had he seen such a crowd in his home park—47,797. Every seat was taken, every inch of standing room filled.

Zoilo felt the tension building as the band finished the national anthem. Even though he had played five full seasons of major league baseball, he still was as excited as the day he had been given his first glove.

But once home plate umpire Ed Hurley called, "Play ball!" Zoilo relaxed. Now all he had to do was think about the game. He wet his lips, pounded his glove, and began his familiar chatter.

"Hubba-hubba-hubba-*cat!*" he called out to Mudcat Grant. And Versalles kept yelling throughout the game —in which he blasted a big homer and drove in four runs. The Twins swept past Drysdale for an easy 8–2 win. Minnesota fans went wild.

If the Twins surprised some people in the baseball world by defeating Don Drysdale in the opening game, they shocked everybody by grinding out a 5–1 win in the second game over the great Sandy Koufax. In that one, Zoilo contributed a booming triple in the seventh inning. His base running so upset relief pitcher Ron Perranoski of the Dodgers that Ron gave him a wild pitch that inning to produce Zoilo's second run of the day.

A grim Dodger team returned to Chavez Stadium and evened the Series, two games to two, downing the Twins, 4–0 and 7–2. Zoilo chipped in with three more hits in these games, but the rest of the Minnesota big bats remained idle. The victories went to Claude Osteen and Don Drysdale.

The fifth game also went to Los Angeles, 7–0, with Koufax spinning a tight four-hit shut out and striking out ten. Even Versalles, the hero of the Series up to now, went without a hit.

The teams returned to Bloomington, with the pressure squarely on the Twins and Jim Grant. It proved to be one of Mudcat's great performances. Not only did he beat the Dodgers, 5–1, to even the Series at three games each, but he hit a three-run home run in the sixth inning. He could have been elected governor of Minnesota on the spot.

Zoilo slept very little the night before the deciding game. He had had a fine record so far, having collected seven hits in twenty-four times at bat, including a double, a triple, and a home run. And he had played errorless ball in the field.

On the day of the final game, Thursday, October 14, Zoilo had a light breakfast. He was too keyed up to eat much, and spent the rest of the morning playing with his four little girls, Amparito, Esthersita, Angela, and Luz Maria, called Lucy for short. Only the oldest could tell that her daddy was involved in some kind of important game.

"Watch out for my right shoulder," Zoilo warned, as he played with her on the living room floor. "Daddy may need it for the game this afternoon." Just then the local radio station cut in with a sports bulletin.

"Manager Walt Alston has announced that his pitcher for this afternoon's game will be Sandy Koufax. The Twins, of course, will go with Jim Kaat, as announced earlier by Sam Mele."

Zoilo rolled over on his back. Koufax! The Dodger lefty was coming back to pitch with only two days' rest. "Maybe he won't have his good stuff," he told Maria as he prepared to leave for the ball park.

Sandy didn't. His curve wasn't breaking. But there was nothing wrong with his fast ball or his slider. Going into the third inning, the score was o–o with both Koufax and Kaat pitching well.

Zoilo came up to face Sandy for the second time in the third inning. From the batter's box, he saw the tired lines on the pitcher's handsome face. Zoilo knew his job was to get the Dodger ace out of there as soon as possible. He did his best by singling sharply to left. The home crowd roared.

The next moment they were screaming wildly as Versalles stole second. But their cheers turned to moans as plate umpire Ed Hurley waved the runner back to first.

Vince Scully, the regular Los Angeles announcer, gave the explanation to the radio and TV audience across the nation. "Umpire Hurley has just ruled that batter Joe Nossek interfered with catcher Roseboro's throw. Versalles is going back to first, and manager Sam Mele is coming out of the dug out."

The Twins' protests were in vain. The decision stood. A moment later Tony Oliva struck out to end the inning.

The call must have upset pitcher Jim Kaat. In the top of the fourth, he fed a home run ball to Lou Johnson, then was tapped for a double and a single, good enough to score another run. Red Worthington was sent in to take Kaat's place with the Dodgers leading, 2–0.

Minnesota fans settled back. It was still early in the ball game. Plenty of time for the Twins to come back. After all, they had been doing just that all season long.

In the fifth inning, Twin second baseman Frank Quilici boomed a long double off the left field wall. Rich Rollins, batting for Worthington, walked. The capacity home crowd cheered. The Twins *were* coming back! In the Dodger bull pen, Don Drysdale began to warm up again, something he had been doing since the first inning.

"Blast it, Zoilo! Pick out a good one, Zee!"

The fans shouted themselves hoarse as a grim Ver-

135

salles stepped up to the plate. A hit now would score a run. More important, it would knock Koufax out of the box. Zoilo gripped the bat, waiting for his pitch. On the mound, Koufax stared back at the batter. For all the noise in the stadium, the two of them might have been the only ones in the ball park.

The runners edged off their bases. Zoilo dug in, swinging his bat. Dodger third baseman Junior Gilliam took a step into the infield. He knew it wasn't beyond the fast short stop to lay down a bunt and beat it out for a hit.

"Ball one!" umpire Hurley called, as Koufax sent a slider wide of the plate.

Manager Mele, standing on the top step of the dug out, bowed his head. Coach Billy Martin shrilled from his third base coaching post. In the stands, Maria Versalles tugged at her lower lip.

"Ball two!"

Zoilo stepped out of the batter's box. Koufax was weary, no question about it. Don Drysdale continued to warm up in the bull pen. The next pitch would have to come over the plate. Koufax knew it. Versalles knew it. A walk at this point would be fatal for the Dodgers.

Zoilo got a fresh grip on his bat. His eyes, behind the tinted glasses, never left Sandy's pitching arm. He saw it go up, back, then down, and over hand—!

The ball came in fast and over the inside corner, belt high. Zoilo jumped on it, snapping the bat around in a powerful swing. The sweet sound of bat on ball cut through the afternoon air—*whack!*

It was a screaming ball, blazing down the third base line on one hop and well to Junior Gilliam's right. It had double stamped all over it, a true Versalles' smash. Zoilo took off for first like a shot. Both base runners leaped forward.

But the quickest man on the field just then was thirty-seven-year-old Junior Gilliam. Making a desperate try, the Dodger third baseman threw his gloved hand across his body. *Whump!* The ball rested in the pocket of his mitt for an easy—and surprising—force out at third.

Zoilo could not believe his eyes. Gilliam had made an impossible clutch play. Zippy took small comfort in the fact that he himself had robbed other hitters with just such plays.

Gilliam's sparkling catch seemed to put new energy into the sagging Koufax. From then on, he reared back and let fly with his high, hard one. The game ended 2–0, and a sad hush fell over Metropolitan Stadium.

The Minnesota Twins had dropped the World Series to the Los Angeles Dodgers, four games to three.

A month later, the annual dinner, given by owner Cal Griffith for his Minnesota club, was held. At it, Cal reminded local fans that few had given the Twins any chance to finish in the first division of the American

League, let alone to become its champions. "But we surprised them, we did," the club owner said. "And we finished right behind the Dodgers in the World Series by a margin no wider than the length of Junior Gilliam's glove."

The audience laughed. The pain of that key play had now worn off. Even Zoilo, his white teeth flashing in a big smile, joined in the fun.

Cal Griffith then held up his hand for silence. "My next announcement," he went on, "should wipe away any last doubts as to why the Minnesota Twins won the pennant this year. I've just received word from the commissioner's office of the choice for the Most Valuable Player in the American League for 1965—" He turned his eyes to the table where the smiling short stop was sitting with his wife. "The choice is Zoilo Versalles of the Minnesota Twins!"

Cheers broke out. The fans knew they had a winner in the former kid from Cuba, but they wanted the whole baseball world to share that knowledge with them.

"This is the year," writer Max Nichols of the Minneapolis *Star* told the dinner audience later, "that Zoilo became the senior short stop in the American League. This is the year that he carried the Twins on his strong, if not broad, shoulders when Harmon Killebrew was injured. This is the year that the Minnesota Twins have a champion among many champions!"

138

"And this is the year," Billy Martin joked, "when Zippy Zee made me the smartest coach in the American League."

When it came to the guest of honor's turn to speak, a hush fell over the crowd. He stood there silent for a moment. He was thinking, just then, of the dusty streets of Marianao, of the first baseball glove given to him by Carlos Paula, of the two *pesetas* bus fare, and of those terrible days of hunger when there wasn't enough to eat for himself or his family.

"I am just lucky," he admitted, standing before the two-foot-high Most Valuable Player prize. "Lucky to get a base hit, lucky to get a home run, lucky to steal a base and—lucky to be here!"

To which a grateful Sam Mele responded: "And we are the luckiest of all—because we have a player like Zoilo Versalles!"

But the best plans of mice and men—even the league's most valuable player—often go wrong. No sooner had the 1966 season started than Zoilo was laid low by an attack of the flu.

As a result his batting suffered. He hit below .200 for the first eight weeks of the campaign. With the team's spark plug below par, the Twins also suffered. They wallowed in the second division as spring gave way to summer.

Nor was Zoilo the lone offender. The pitchers didn't pitch well and the batters didn't hit. Meanwhile, the Baltimore Orioles, led by Frank and Brooks Robinson, zoomed to the top of the American League.

"Things have to get better," muttered manager Sam Mele. "Maybe after the All-Star break."

But things got worse, for the team as well as for Zoilo Versalles. A heel injury forced the short stop to the sidelines early in July. He missed three weeks of play while his foot slowly healed. The Twins dropped to seventh place, then to eighth.

Zoilo finally returned to the line-up early in August. He moved around gingerly at first, afraid that his heel might act up again. But it didn't. Soon he was Zippy Zee all over again, covering the short field with all his former speed.

His return seemed to spark the rest of the team. Jim Kaat, now the ace of the mound staff, put together a half dozen good games in a row. Mudcat Grant settled down. Killebrew and Earl Battey began to hit. So did Zoilo.

The Twins started their long climb back as contenders. They won one series after another, knocking off the league-leading Orioles, the Detroit Tigers, and the White Sox. The Yankees, once their most feared rivals, proved the easiest prey of all. By Labor Day, the Twins had fought their way into the first division.

But there was no catching the Baltimore Orioles. They went into September with a ten-game lead and clinched the American League flag soon after the middle of the month. Now it became a three-way battle for second place among the Tigers, White Sox, and the Twins.

With their hitting, pitching, and speed working to perfection, the Minnesota club swept past the rest of the league. But after the team's poor start, due in part to Zoilo's early season injury, the best the Twins could do was finish in second place, nine games behind the Orioles.

In spite of a fine second half in 1966, it was not one of Zoilo's better seasons. He finished the campaign with 543 at bats, about a hundred fewer than normal. He scored 74 runs and had only 135 hits, since he had missed more than twenty games. His final batting average was .249, well behind his career record.

"If only I could toss out the first half of the season," Zoilo sighed as he cleaned out his locker. "I might have hit .300."

Billy Martin looked up from across the way. "Then it would have been us, and not Baltimore, that would meet the Dodgers in the World Series."

"Well, at least we can root for the American League team," Zoilo answered. "I'm going home right now, put my feet up, and watch the Series . . . on television!"

It proved to be a great Series . . . for American League fans. The Orioles took four straight from the Los

Angeles Dodgers in one of the biggest upsets of the sports world.

After the last game, Zoilo leaned over and turned off his TV set. "More problems," he said quietly to himself.

He was already looking ahead to next season, figuring out ways to hit against the Orioles' young mound staff which had hurled three straight World Series shut outs at the Dodgers.